NORMAN E. GRONLUND
UNIVERSITY OF ILLINOIS

Stating Objectives for Classroom Instruction

3RD EDITION

Macmillan Publishing Company New York
Collier Macmillan Publishers London

Macmillan Publishing Company
866 Third Avenue, New York, New York 10022

Collier Macmillan Canada, Inc.

ISBN 0-02-348000-9

Printing: 2 3 4 5 6 7 8   Year: 5 6 7 8 9

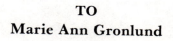

TO
Marie Ann Gronlund

Preface

This is a practical guide for preparing instructional objectives for use in classroom instruction. It describes how to state instructional objectives as intended learning outcomes and how to define the objectives in terms of student performance. That is, in terms of what students can do to demonstrate that they have learned. The procedures are illustrated throughout with sample objectives and statements of specific learning outcomes. The role of instructional objectives in teaching, testing, evaluation, and marking and reporting is also described and illustrated.

The organization of the book has been modified somewhat from the earlier edition, and now is as follows:

- The first four chapters provide step-by-step directions for preparing a list of instructional objectives.
- Chapter 5 describes and illustrates how to use the *Taxonomy of Educational Objectives* in preparing instructional objectives.
- Chapters 6-9 show how to use instructional objectives in teaching, preparing tests, evaluating performance and affective outcomes, and marking and reporting.
- Appendixes provide a checklist for evaluating objectives and a list of verbs classified by types of learning outcome.

This third edition includes a number of changes from the last edition.

- Chapters 3 and 4 were combined and new material was added.
- A new Chapter 4 was written to describe how to prepare the final list of objectives. Material from Chapter 6 was incorporated into this chapter.
- Sample objectives in various content areas were added to Chapters 1-4.
- Illustrative specifications for preparing test items for computer item banking were added to Chapter 7.

The basic approach to preparing instructional objectives remains the same as in the earlier editions. It focuses on statements of objectives that are general enough to provide guides for both teaching and testing, without restricting the freedom of the teacher, and specific enough to clearly indicate the types of performance students are to demonstrate when they have achieved the objectives. This approach provides for the inclusion of learning outcomes of all types—ranging from the simplest to the most complex—and it is useful at all levels of instruction.

I am indebted to Ralph Tyler and his coworkers for their preparation of the *Taxonomy of Educational Objectives,* to Calvin K. Claus for his preparation of the useful list of verbs in Appendix B, and to Lloyd C. Chilton and the Macmillan editorial staff for their valuable help in preparing this edition.

N. E. G.

List of Tables

Contents

Chapter 1

Instructional Objectives
as Learning Outcomes

"Why Use Objectives in Teaching?"

Although much has been written about instructional objectives over the years, some teachers still ask this question. Numerous specific answers could be given, but basically they can be combined into the three purposes depicted below.

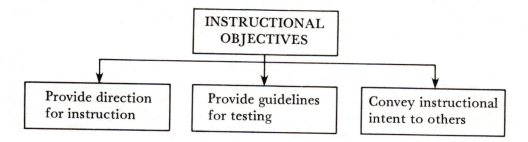

These purposes are best served, however, when the objectives are properly stated as intended learning outcomes of the instruction.

Focusing on Intended Learning Outcomes

There are, of course, many different ways of stating instructional objectives. One common type of statement is in terms of what we, as teachers, are going to do. Thus, we might have a statement like the following:

To demonstrate to students how to set up laboratory equipment.

The difficulty with a statement like this is that it focuses attention on the teaching activity rather than on the learning outcomes to be attained by the students. Literally speaking, we have achieved the objective once we have completed the demonstration—whether or not the students have learned anything from it. A more fruitful way to state instructional objectives is in terms of the types of outcomes we expect from our teaching; therefore, after we demonstrate how to use laboratory equipment, we might expect students to be able to do the following:

1.   Identify the laboratory equipment used in the demonstration.
2.   Describe the steps to be followed in setting up the laboratory equipment.
3.   List the necessary precautions in handling and setting up the laboratory equipment.
4.   Demonstrate skills in setting up their own laboratory equipment.

When instructional objectives are stated like this, they direct attention to the students and to the types of performance students are expected to exhibit as a result of the learning experience. Our focus thus shifts from the teacher to the students and from the learning *process* to the learning *outcomes.* This shift clarifies the intent of our instruction and provides the basis for an evaluation of student learning.

The distinction between stating objectives in terms of what you are going to do as a teacher and stating them in terms of the learning outcomes you expect from your students is an important one. To check on your grasp of this distinction, look at the following two objectives and decide which one is stated as an expected learning outcome.[1]

1.   Instills an understanding of the scientific method.
2.   Distinguishes between valid and invalid conclusions.

You should have selected the second objective, which clearly specifies how students will demonstrate, at the end of the instructional period, that they have learned. Note that the statement begins with a verb that implies an activity on the part of the student. There is no need to add such refinements as "The student has the ability to *distinguish*," "The student can *distinguish*," or "The student should be able to demonstrate that he or she can *distinguish*." The less wordy the objective, the better. Our aim is to indicate clearly the intent of our instruction in terms of the type of response (*distinguishes between*) that the student is expected to show.

The word *instills* in the first statement implies that the teacher, not the student, is engaging in an activity. By omitting this word, you can restate this objective in terms of a learning outcome, as follows:

---

[1] Throughout this book you will be presented with opportunities for self-testing. To benefit most, you should choose between alternatives before you continue your reading.

Understands the scientific method.

Note that although this objective is now stated as an outcome, the term *understands* is much more general than the term *distinguishes between*. To indicate clearly the intent of our instruction, it would be necessary to further define this objective by listing the specific types of student performance we are willing to accept as evidence of their understanding. This process of stating general objectives and then of further defining them in terms of specific statements has some advantage over the use of single statements of objectives, as we shall see shortly. First, however, let's see if we can further clarify the meaning of "instructional objectives as learning outcomes" by taking a look at their role in the instructional process.

Learning Outcomes and the Instructional Process

The relation of learning outcomes to the learning experiences provided during the teaching-learning phase of instruction is shown in Figure 1.

Student →	TEACHING–LEARNING PROCESS →	LEARNING OUTCOMES (End Products)
	(Learning experiences based on interaction of subject matter, teaching methods, and instructional materials)	Knowledge Understanding Application Thinking skills Performance skills Computer skills Communication skills Computational skills Work-study skills Social skills Attitudes Interests Appreciation Adjustments

FIGURE 1. Relation of learning outcomes to learning experiences.

This diagram makes clear the fact that the learning experiences provided during the teaching-learning process are not ends in themselves but means to ends. The subject matter, the teaching methods, and materials used in instruction are to be viewed as tools to bring about desired learning outcomes.

Although the diagram appears simple, the *process* of instruction and the *products* of instruction are frequently confused in statements of instructional objectives. For example, which one of the following objectives is stated as a *product* (i.e., a learning *outcome*)?

1.   Increases proficiency in the use of charts and graphs.
2.   Interprets charts and graphs.

You are correct if you selected the second objective, which describes in general terms what the student does at the end of the learning experience. We later would want to clarify further what we mean by *interprets* (e.g., identifies a given point on a graph, describes the trend shown in a graph, etc.), but this instructional objective is definitely stated as a learning *product*.

In the first statement the term *increases* provides a clue that we are concerned here with a *process*. The statement doesn't clarify how the student is to demonstrate his or her increased proficiency at the end of the instruction. Is the student to interpret charts and graphs, to construct charts and graphs, or to give a speech in which charts and graphs will be used as visual aids? Stating objectives in terms of the learning *process* is misleading because one learning experience may contribute to many different learning outcomes, and one learning outcome (e.g., a scientific attitude) may be the result of many different learning experiences.

The first step in instructional planning, then, should be to identify and define our instructional objectives as learning outcomes. When we specify the types of performance (i.e., knowledge, understanding, skills, etc.) that we expect students to be able to demonstrate at the end of instruction, we can more wisely select the materials and methods of instruction. The statements of intended outcomes also clarify the specific types of performance to be tested when evaluating student learning and can be used to convey our instructional intent to students, parents, and others who might be interested.

Stating Instructional Objectives As Learning Outcomes

As noted earlier, there are two ways of stating objectives as learning outcomes. One is to list each specific type of performance students are to exhibit at the end of the instructional period. For example, we might start a list as follows:

1.   Defines each technical term in his or her own words.
2.   Identifies the meaning of each technical term when used in context.
3.   Distinguishes between technical terms that are similar in meaning.

A second method is to state first the general instructional objectives and then to clarify each objective by listing a *sample* of the specific types of student performance we are willing to accept as evidence of the attainment of that objective. This procedure would result in statements such as the following:

1. Understands the meaning of technical terms.
    1.1 Defines the term in his or her own words.
    1.2 Identifies the meaning of the term when used in context.
    1.3 Distinguishes between terms that are similar in meaning.

Note that the specific statements are the same in both instances. The first list, however, implies that these types of performance are ends in themselves and that instruction is to be given directly in the specified performance. For example, we teach students "to define a technical term in their own words"; then, to test achievement of the outcome, we ask them "to define the technical term in their own words." This one-to-one relationship between the performance taught and the performance tested is characteristic of the training level and is widely used in programmed instruction. For regular classroom instruction, however, this procedure is useful only for teaching the simplest skills and the lowest levels of knowledge (see Box 1).

Stating the general instructional objective first and then clarifying it further by listing the specific types of performance that characterize the objective is more than a matter of literary form. This procedure makes clear that the instructional objective is *understanding* and not *defining, identifying,* or *distinguishing between.* These latter terms simply describe a *sample of the types of performance that represent understanding.* A different sample

---

1. WHY NOT INCLUDE CONDITIONS AND STANDARDS?

It is sometimes suggested that in addition to describing the desired *student performance*, an objective should include the *conditions* under which the performance is to be demonstrated and the *standard* of performance to be accepted. This method of stating objectives would result in a statement as follows (each element is identified to the left of the statement):

Condition	Given a drawing of a flower
Performance	The student will label in writing
Standard	At least 4 of the 5 parts shown.

Statements such as this are especially useful for programmed instruction and for mastery testing in simple training programs. When used for regular classroom instruction, however, they result in long cumbersome lists that restrict the freedom of the teacher. If we restated the above as "Identifies the parts of a given plant structure" it could be used with various units of study and the teacher would be free to use real plants, pictures, diagrams, slides, or other stimulus material. Also, the students could respond orally, in writing, or simply by pointing to a named part. The standard (in this case 80%) could be set at the time of testing, either for the whole test or separately for each part. Keeping the standard separate from the objective makes it possible to vary the standards as needed without rewriting the objectives. For example, we may want to set lower standards at the beginning of a unit of study and higher standards at the end. Similarly we may want to set higher standards for a gifted group and lower standards for a retarded group. Let's not waste time rewriting objectives to fit changing conditions.

of specific types of performance could serve equally well. For example, we might use the following list instead of the one cited earlier.

1.   Understands the meaning of technical terms.
     1.1 Relates technical terms to the concepts they represent.
     1.2 Uses each term in an original sentence.
     1.3 Identifies similarities and differences between terms.

Note that the instructional objective is still *understanding*. We have merely listed a new sample of student performance to characterize what is meant by the statement *understands the meaning of technical terms*. It would be impossible to list all types of performance that might show understanding; therefore, we must settle for a representative sample.

The fact that the specific learning outcomes simply serve as *samples* of the types of performance we are willing to accept as evidence of the attainment of our general instructional objectives has implications for both teaching and testing. Our teaching efforts must be directed toward the general objectives of instruction and not toward the specific samples of performance we have selected to represent each objective. For example, in teaching an *understanding of technical terms,* we might have the students study the textbook definitions, compare and contrast the terms during class discussion, and use the terms in their laboratory work. When we test the students, however, we present them with a list of technical terms and ask them to define each term in their own words and to write an original sentence using the term. Note that the test calls for a type of response that was not directly taught during classroom instruction. This is necessary if the test results are to show an *understanding* rather than merely a *recall* of previous learning. Also the test calls forth only a sample of the types of performance that might be used to represent an *understanding of technical terms*. It would be impractical to include test items that measure all aspects of understanding, just as it would be impractical to include all technical terms in a particular test. In both cases we must be satisfied with a sample—a sample of the many terms that the students have studied during instruction, and a sample of the many types of performance that could be used as evidence of the students' understanding of terms. If our samples are carefully chosen, we can then generalize from our test results to the larger achievement domain. That is, we can estimate how well the students have achieved our instructional objective, the *understanding of technical terms* (see Box 2).

In summary, when instruction is concerned with a simple task, it may be possible to list all of the types of performance that are involved in the task, to teach these types of performance directly, and to include them all in an evaluation of student learning at the end of instruction. This method is characteristic of the teaching-learning process at the training level. For higher levels of instruction, however, it is possible to list only a *sample* of the specific types of student performance that represent each instructional

2. SOME BASIC TERMINOLOGY

General Instructional Objective	An intended outcome of instruction that has been stated in general enough terms to encompass a domain of student performance (e.g., Comprehends the literal meaning of written material). A general instructional objective must be further defined by a set of specific learning outcomes to clarify instructional intent.
Specific Learning Outcome	An intended outcome of instruction that has been stated in terms of specific and observable *student performance* (e.g., Identifies details that are explicitly stated in a passage). Specific learning outcomes describe the types of performance that learners will be able to exhibit when they have achieved a general instructional objective (specific learning outcomes are also called Specific Objectives. Performance Objectives, and Measurable Objectives).
Student Performance	Any measurable or observable student response that is a result of learning.

objective. This list provides a guide for both teaching and testing, but it is obvious that instruction should not focus on the particular sample listed but rather on the larger achievement domain that the sample represents. The necessity for sampling at the higher levels of learning makes it desirable to define learning outcomes in a two-step process.

1. To state the general instructional objectives as learning outcomes.
2. To list, under each instructional objective, a representative sample of the specific learning outcomes that indicate attainment of the objective.

In Chapter 2 we shall describe how to state clearly the general instructional objectives, and in Chapter 3 we shall describe how to define each objective in more specific terms. In Chapter 4 we shall pull it all together and describe the complete process for preparing a set of objectives for classroom instruction.

Chapter 2

Stating the General Instructional Objectives

The first step in defining instructional objectives is to state the general learning outcomes we expect from our teaching. This step sounds simple enough, but most teachers find it difficult. They tend to focus on the teaching process, the learning process, or on the subject matter, rather than on the expected *outcomes* of instruction. Teachers also have some difficulty stating the objectives at a satisfactory level of generality; that is, of striking a happy medium between broad, undefinable statements and long, unmanageable lists of specific types of behavior. Let's first take a look at some of the common errors to avoid in stating instructional objectives.

Avoiding Errors in Stating the General Objectives

One of the most common errors in stating objectives has already been considered—that of describing teacher performance rather than student performance. Look at the following two objectives, for example, and note the difference in how they are stated. Which one most clearly indicates an instructional outcome?

1. Comprehends assigned reading material.
2. To increase the student's reading ability.

You should have had little difficulty in selecting between these two statements. The first statement contains an expected outcome of instruction. Later we would need to list a sample of the specific types of performance that we are willing to accept as evidence that the student *comprehends,* but as stated this is a good general outcome.

The second statement gives a less clear picture of the intended results of instruction. It also gives the psychologically unsound impression that it is the teacher who is going to do the increasing rather than the student.

Another common error was also mentioned in Chapter 1; that is, stating an objective in terms of the learning *process* rather than as a learning *product*. The following two statements will clarify the difference. Which one is stated as a *product* of instruction, i.e., an instructional *outcome*?

1. Gains knowledge of basic principles.
2. Applies basic principles to new situations.

If you selected the second statement, you are correct. This statement clearly indicates what the student can do at the end of instruction. The first statement emphasizes the gaining of knowledge (learning *process*) rather than the type of performance that provides evidence that learning has taken place. Words like *gains, acquires,* and *develops* give away the fact that an objective is focused on the learning *process* rather than on the expected *outcome* of the learning experience.

In some cases where objectives are stated in terms of the learning *process*, the instructional intent is still fairly clear. This is frequently true for simple learning outcomes. For example, in the statement *develops skill in adding whole numbers,* the learning outcome is quite obvious. In other cases, however, a single learning experience might contribute to any number of learning outcomes, none of which is readily apparent in the statement of objectives. For example, look at the following statement.

Learns symbols on a weather map.

This statement does clarify what the student is to learn, but it does not clarify the learning *outcomes* toward which the student should be directed. The teacher who wrote this statement might have in mind any one of the following learning outcomes:

Recalls the symbols used on a weather map.
Identifies the symbols on a weather map.
Interprets a weather map (using the symbols).
Constructs a weather map (using the symbols).
Predicts weather from a weather map (using the symbols).

It is obvious that the statement *learns symbols* does not indicate the intent of the instruction so clearly as the statements of learning *outcomes* listed above. Identifying the nature of the desired product provides greater direction for planning, carrying out, and evaluating the learning experiences.

Another common error in stating objectives is simply to list the subject matter to be covered. This error is readily apparent in a comparison of the following two statements. Which one is properly stated?

1. Principles of electricity.
2. Understands basic principles.

The correct answer is, of course, the second statement. The first statement consists of no more than a subject-matter topic. There is no indication of what the students are expected to do with regard to the principles of electricity. Are students simply to know them, to understand them, or to apply them in some way?

The second statement could read *understands principles of electricity,* but there is some advantage in broadening the statement to include all types of principles covered in the instruction. The same outcome can then be used to indicate the expected reaction to any principle studied. When this is done, the specific types of student response used to clarify what is meant by the word *understands* must, of course, be *performance* oriented rather than *content* oriented. When complete, the statement of the objective and of the specific learning *outcomes* might appear as follows:

Understands Basic Principles

1. States the principle in his or her own words.
2. Identifies an example of the principle.
3. Distinguishes between correct and incorrect applications of the principle.

Note that the specific statements do not indicate what principles the students are to understand, but rather what *performance* they are to demonstrate as evidence that they understand. By not including a reference to subject matter in statements of learning *outcomes,* you can develop a set of outcomes that is useful with various units of instruction throughout a course. Thus the subject matter in each unit of instruction will indicate the principles that are to be studied, and the learning *outcomes* will indicate the types of reactions the students are to make to the principles.

Another common error is to include more than one type of learning *outcome* in each general objective. Look at the following two statements. Which one contains a *single outcome?*

1. Uses appropriate experimental procedures in solving problems.
2. Knows the scientific method and applies it effectively.

Of course the answer is 1. The second statement includes both *knows* and *applies* as possible *outcomes.* It is better to have a separate statement for each because some students may know the scientific method (i.e., be able to describe it) but may not be able to apply it effectively. With separate statements, you can define each objective in terms of specific learning outcomes and thus determine how well each objective is being achieved.

In this section we have focused on the common errors to avoid in stating the general instructional objectives. These errors include stating the objectives in terms of (1) the teacher's performance, (2) the learning process, (3) the subject matter, and (4) a combination of two or more outcomes. These errors can be avoided by *focusing attention on the student and on the type of performance he or she is expected to demonstrate at the end of instruction.* Instructional objectives, then, should be brief, clear statements that describe instructional intent in terms of the desired learning *outcomes* (see Box 1).

In addition to avoiding the common errors in stating instructional objectives, one of the most difficult tasks is to select the proper level of generality in stating each major objective.

Selecting the Proper Level of Generality

When developing a list of general instructional objectives for a course (or unit of course work), our aim is to obtain a list of outcomes to work toward and not a list of specific tasks to be performed by all students. To be sure, each general instructional objective will need to be defined further by a sample of the specific types of student performance that characterize each objective, but at this stage we are focusing only on the stating of the general objectives.

---

1. STATING INSTRUCTIONAL OBJECTIVES

1. Don't state them in terms of *teacher performance.* (e.g., Teach students scientific concepts.)
2. Don't state them in terms of the *learning process.* (e.g., Student learns scientific concepts.)
3. Don't focus on the *subject matter* topics. (e.g., Student learns the meaning of osmosis, photosynthesis, etc.)
4. Don't include two objectives in one statement. (e.g., Student knows and understands scientific concepts.)

State and define each objective in terms of the type of *student performance* that is to be demonstrated at the end of instruction, as illustrated below:

1. Understands scientific concepts.
   1.1 Defines the concept.
   1.2 Identifies an example of the concept.
   1.3 States hypotheses based on the concept.
   1.4 Describes how the process functions in a given situation.
   1.5 Describes an experiment that illustrates the process.

You may have noticed by now that each of the instructional objectives used in this chapter to illustrate properly stated learning outcomes began with a verb. The following verbs were used in these statements.

Applies
Comprehends
Knows
Understands
Uses

These verbs provide a clue to the desired level of generality for our major objectives. They are specific enough to provide direction for instruction without overly restricting the teacher or reducing the instruction to the training level. They are also specific enough to be easily defined by a brief list of the types of performance students are to demonstrate when the objectives have been achieved.

Let's look at a few sample statements that illustrate the problem of selecting a proper level of generality. Which one of the following statements represents the most general objective? Which one the most specific?

1.   Communicates effectively in English.
2.   Writes clear, effective English.
3.   Punctuates sentences properly.

The first statement represents the most general objective. In fact, it is probably too general for a major objective because communication includes speaking, listening, writing, and reading. Each of these areas is general enough to provide a major objective by itself.

The most specific is 3, which might be a good specific learning outcome to be listed under a more general objective, but it is probably too specific to be used as a general instructional objective. Thus the second statement comes closest to the desired level of generality. It clearly indicates the general nature of the expected learning *outcome,* and it can be defined by a relatively short, clear list of specific learning outcomes.

The degree of generality in the list of major objectives will, of course, vary with the period of instruction for which the list is being prepared. The objectives for an entire course will, of necessity, be more general than those for a unit of instruction within the course. Teachers typically find that from eight to twelve general instructional objectives are sufficient for a course of instruction and from two to four for a brief instructional unit (see Box 2).

Summary of Procedure for Stating General Instructional Objectives

In summary, use the following suggestions as a guide for stating the general instructional objectives.

1. State each general instructional objective as an *intended learning outcome* (i.e., students' *terminal performance*).
2. Begin each general objective with a verb that is general enough to encompass a domain of student performance (e.g., *knows, understands, applies*). Omit "The student is able to. . . ."
3. State each general objective so that it includes only one general learning outcome (rather than combining several outcomes).
4. Keep the statements relatively free of *specific* subject matter (so they can be used with various instructional units).
5. State each general objective at a level of generality that is readily definable by a set of specific learning outcomes. Including from eight to twelve general general instructional objectives for a course of instruction will usually suffice. For a brief unit of instruction, from two to four general objectives may be enough.

SOME SAMPLE GENERAL INSTRUCTIONAL OBJECTIVES

Reading

1. Knows word meanings.
2. Comprehends the literal meaning of written material.
3. Infers meaning from written material.
4. Interprets tables, graphs, maps and diagrams.
5. Evaluates written material using specific criteria (e.g., realistic, accurate).
6. Adapts reading rate to material and purpose of reading.
7. Locates information by using guides (e.g., index, table of contents, reference works).
8. Demonstrates a positive attitude toward reading.

Mathematics

1. Knows the meaning of terms and symbols.
2. Computes accurately and rapidly.
3. Understands mathematical concepts and processes.
4. Understands the number systems.
5. Applies concepts and processes to mathematical problems.
6. Invents new mathematical applications or generalizations.
7. Interprets measuring instruments, tables, and graphs.
8. Demonstrates a positive attitude toward mathematics.

Science

1. Knows the meaning of terms.
2. Knows specific facts.
3. Knows laboratory procedures.
4. Understands concepts and principles.
5. Applies concepts and principles to new situations.
6. Demonstrates skills and abilities needed to conduct an experiment.
7. Interprets data in scientific reports.
8. Displays a scientific attitude.

Chapter 3

Stating the Specific Learning Outcomes

When you have prepared a tentative list of general instructional objectives, you are ready to define each general objective in terms of the specific types of student performance that you are willing to accept as evidence that the objective has been achieved. These *specific learning outcomes* provide an operational definition of what we mean when we state that a student "knows terms", "understands principles," or "interprets charts and graphs." Unless the general objectives are further clarified in this way, they will convey only a fuzzy notion of the intended outcomes of instruction.

Stating the Specific Outcomes in Terms of Student Performance

The following statement of a general instructional objective and list of specific learning outcomes illustrates what is meant by defining instructional objectives in terms of *student performance*.

Knows Specific Facts (American History)

1. Identifies important dates, events, places, and persons.
2. Describes the characteristics of a given historical period.
3. Lists important events in chronological order.
4. Relates events to their most probable causes.

Note that each specific learning outcome starts with an *action verb* that indicates *observable* student responses; that is, responses that can be seen by an outside observer. These verbs are listed as follows in order to clarify the types of terms needed for stating the specific learning outcomes.

Identifies
Describes
Lists
Relates

These verbs describe the types of responses the students are to exhibit as evidence that they have achieved the general instructional objective *knows specific facts.* As noted earlier, the above types of response provide only a sample of the specific outcomes that could be included under this objective. The list might be lengthened, shortened, or radically modified to fit the emphasis of a particular course. As an instructor you must define your own instructional objectives in terms of the specific learning outcomes you deem most appropriate. All we are doing here is illustrating the process of stating the specific outcomes in terms of identifiable student performance.

To check on your ability to distinguish between appropriate and inappropriate terms, look at the following two statements. Which one is stated in terms of student performance?

1. Realizes the importance of neatness.
2. Explains the importance of neatness.

You are correct if you selected the second statement. The term *explains* indicates a response that is definite and clearly observable. The first statement does not specify how students will demonstrate that they *realize* the importance of neatness. Will they give reasons for being neat or will they dress more neatly? Terms such as this are subject to many interpretations and should be avoided when you state the specific learning outcomes for each general objective. Let's try another pair of statements to be sure you can tell the difference between *performance* and *nonperformance* terms. Which one of the following clearly indicates student performance?

1. Predicts the outcome of an experiment.
2. Sees the value of an experiment.

This time you should have had little difficulty in selecting the first statement as the correct answer. The term *sees* is a common one in education (e.g., "I see the point"), and its familiarity might have misled you. But, note that *sees* refers to an internal state. What will the students do when they see the value of an experiment? Will they describe its usefulness, point out its theoretical implications, or estimate the social consequences of the results? We simply can't tell because the term *sees* is vague, indefinite, and describes a reaction that is not directly observable.

In stating specific learning outcomes, then, it is wise to begin each statement with a verb that specifies definite, observable student performance.

Statements beginning with a verb clarify from the outset the types of responses students are expected to make when they have achieved the general objective. Helpful lists of verbs for stating specific learning outcomes are included in Appendix B.

Obtaining a Representative Sample of Specific Learning Outcomes

When defining a general objective with a list of specific learning outcomes, you will need to decide how many specific outcomes to list for each objective. There are no hard-and-fast rules for this. It is obvious that simple knowledge and skill outcomes will require fewer than more complex ones, but even relatively simple instructional objects may encompass such a large number of specific types of performance that only a small proportion of them can be listed. Take "Knowledge of terms," for example, and note the various types of student performance that might be listed.

Knows the Meaning of Terms

1. Writes a definition of the term.
2. Identifies a definition of the term.
3. Identifies the term that fits a given description.
4. Identifies a synonym of the term.
5. Identifies an antonym of the term.
6. Identifies an example of the term.
7. Identifies the term represented by a symbol (e.g., +, −).
8. Draws a picture that represents the term (e.g., circle, square).
9. Describes the procedure the term represents.
10. States the concept or principle that fits the term.
11. Describes the relationship of the term to a second term.
12. Differentiates between the term and a second term.
13. Differentiates between the technical meaning and the common meaning of the term.
14. Identifies the best meaning of the term when used in a sentence.
15. Distinguishes between proper and improper usage of the term.

Although this list is not exhaustive, it makes clear the futility of attempting to list all of the possible specific types of response that might represent a particular objective. All we can reasonably expect to do is to list a sample of the specific types of performance that the students are expected to demonstrate when they have achieved the objective. The aim is to select as representative a sample as possible, so that students' performance on the selected outcomes will be characteristic of what their performance would be like on similar outcomes encompassed by the same general instructional objective.

The specific outcomes that are most representative of a general instructional objective will be modified by both the nature of the subject taught and the grade level at which the instruction is given. For "Knowing terms", for example, an English teacher would be likely to stress the identification of synonyms, antonyms, the meaning of words in context, and similar outcomes related to reading ability; whereas, a math teacher would emphasize outcomes that relate the meaning of terms to symbols (e.g., X, =), figures (e.g., types of angles), operations (e.g., grouping into *sets*), and the like. Similarly, a primary teacher would be likely to state fewer and simpler types of outcomes based on picture identification and student drawings.

When the instructional objectives are complex, special care is needed to ensure that the key elements are included in the list of specific learning outcomes without making the list too long and unmanageable. For example, let's examine a sample of learning outcomes used to define such a complex objective as the following:

Applies Critical Thinking Skills in Reading

1. Distinguishes between facts and opinions.
2. Distinguishes between facts and inferences.
3. Identifies cause–effect relations.
4. Identifies errors in reasoning.
5. Distinguishes between relevant and irrelevant arguments.
6. Distinguishes between warranted and unwarranted generalizations.
7. Identifies valid conclusions in written material.
8. Identifies assumptions needed to make conclusions true.

Although this list of types of specific outcomes is by no means complete, a careful reading of the statements will provide a fairly good indication of what students are like when they are able to use critical thinking skills in reading. This list thus is comprehensive enough to clarify the instructional intent and yet short enough to be manageable and useful.

To identify the key elements in complex objectives it is often necessary to consult reference books and other relevant materials. You are not likely to find a neat list of outcomes from which to choose, but even general discussions of the concepts involved will help to define the objectives. Thus, when objectives are concerned with *critical thinking, scientific attitude, creativity,* and the like, a trip to the library might be needed.

Complex objectives are difficult to define, but are usually more important from an educational standpoint. Don't overload your list of instructional objectives with simple learning outcomes simply because they are easy to define.

Emphasizing Instructional Intent

The *action verb* is the key element in stating the specific learning outcomes that define each general instructional objective. The selection of action verbs thus is a vital step in the preparation of a useful set of objectives. In general, we should select those verbs that (1) most clearly convey our instructional intent and (2) most precisely specify the student performance we are willing to accept as evidence that the general instructional objective has been achieved. Unfortunately, action verbs vary widely in their ability to meet both criteria.

Some verbs communicate instructional intent well but are less precise concerning the specific response to be observed. Other verbs clearly indicate the performance to be observed, but the indicated response does not satisfactorily convey the intent of the instruction. Let's look at a few examples. Which one of the following most clearly conveys instructional intent? Which one most precisely specifies the performance to be observed?

1. Identifies the parts on a diagram for an electrical circuit.
2. Labels the parts on a diagram for an electrical circuit.

If you selected the first statement as most clearly conveying instructional intent, you are correct. In this particular instance, the focus of our instruction would be on the *identification* of the parts and not the labeling of them. Although the term *labels* is more descriptive of the precise response the students are expected to make, labeling is not the intended learning outcome. We assume students already know how to label. In this instance, we are simply using labeling as one way that identification might be shown. Identification might also be shown by pointing to, touching, marking, matching, circling, underlining, and so on. These *indicators* of "the ability to identify" clearly specify the student performance to be observed, but they do not always make clear the intent of the instruction,

Given a choice between verbs that clearly convey instructional intent and those that merely serve as performance indicators, it is wise to select the former when stating specific learning outcomes. For test construction purposes, it may be desirable to include both by adding a third level of specificity to the set of intended learning outcomes (see Box 1).

For some purposes it may be desirable to clarify specific learning outcomes with sample test items. This is especially useful where the outcomes are to serve as a basis for test construction by a group of teachers (e.g., for a department test). Nothing communicates the expected student response to others so precisely as sample test items. For example, specific outcomes for "knowing terms" might be further clarified as follows:

Identifies a Definition of the Term

1. What is meant by *overt behavior?*
   *A. Behavior that is observable by others.
   B. Behavior that is repeated over and over again.
   C. Behavior that occurs within an individual.
   D. Misbehavior that should be corrected.

Identifies a Synonym of the Term

2. Which of the following terms has the same meaning as *create?*
   A. Acquire
   B. Alter
   C. Initiate
   *D. Originate

Identifies an Antonym of the Term

3. Which one of the following terms means the opposite of *expand?*
   *A. Contract
   B. Divide
   C. Enlarge
   D. Extend

Each sample test item clarifies what is meant by the specific outcome and serves as a model for constructing test items that call forth the intended student response.

Keeping the Statements Relatively Free of Course Content

As with the general instructional objectives, the specific learning out-

---

1. USING THREE LEVELS TO SPECIFY INTENDED LEARNING OUTCOMES

1. Comprehends the meaning of written material.
   1.1 Identifies information that is explicitly stated in a passage.
      1.11 Underlines specific details in the passage (e.g., names, dates, events, etc.).
      1.12 Selects statements that best match the literal meaning of the passage.
      1.13 Lists facts that support the major theme of the passage.
   1.2 Identifies the main thought of a passage.
      1.21 Underlines the topic sentence in the passage.
      1.22 Selects the best title for the passage.
   1.3 Summarizes the ideas in a passage.
      1.31 Writes a condensed version of the passage.
   1.4 Infers ideas and relationships not explicitly stated in a passage.
      1.41 Describes ideas, actions, or events that are implied in the content of the passage.
      1.42 Lists actions or events in the order in which they most likely occurred.
      1.43 Selects the most probable outcome for an action or event that is described in the passage.
      1.44 Explains why objects, ideas, or events should be grouped together.

comes should be kept free of *specific* course content. The following statements, for example, would be too content oriented.

Identifies the parts of the heart.
Identifies the parts of the lung.
Describes the functions of the heart.
Describes the functions of the lung.

For most classroom purposes, it would be more desirable to state the specific learning outcomes as follows:

Identifies the parts of a given structure.
Describes the functions of a given structure.

Statements like these clearly describe what type of performance the students are to demonstrate, but the responses are not tied to a specific body part. In fact, the revised statements would be useful with any animal or plant structure we are studying. The advantage of keeping the statements content free is, of course, that a set of objectives can then be used with various units of study. The subject-matter topics in each unit specify the content the student is to react to, and the specific learning outcomes describe the types of reactions to be made by the students.

To be sure you grasp the distinction being made here, look at the following pair of learning outcomes and decide which one would be most useful with various units of study:

Lists the major battles of World War II in chronological order.
Lists historical events in chronological order.

It is rather obvious that the second one is a common learning outcome that can be used repeatedly in a history course. This statement also illustrates that keeping the stated outcomes content free is a matter of degree. Sometimes all we need to do is substitute generalized content (e.g., historical events) for specific content (e.g., World War II). Thus, when we find ourselves listing specific tasks like the following, we might simply combine them into a single statement like "Distinguishes among geometric shapes."

Distinguishes between a circle and a square.
Distinguishes between a square and a rectangle.
Distinguishes between a rectangle and a triangle.

There is nothing basically wrong with combining the student responses and specific course content in the same statement. In fact, it would probably be desirable when preparing materials for programmed instruction or when dealing with some limited type of training program. However, when used for regular classroom instruction, the inclusion of specific course content in each statement results in the repetitious writing of objectives as each new subject-matter topic is considered. This time might be better spent in developing instructional materials in preparing valid tests, and in doing other instructional tasks.

Making Sure the Specific Learning Outcomes Are Relevant

It goes without saying that each specific learning outcome should be relevant to the instructional objective it is defining, but this criterion constitutes another area of difficulty in listing the specific statements. Look at the following two statements, for example. Which one should be listed under the general goal *understands scientific principles?*

1. Makes a prediction using the principle.
2. States the textbook definition of the principle.

Given a choice between these two, we would have to select the first. The second statement implies no more than the simple recall of information and therefore would be best classified as a *knowledge* outcome. The first statement goes beyond the recall of previously learned facts and asks the student to use the principle in a way that reflects an understanding of its meaning.

The problem is not quite that simple, however. Since knowledge is a prerequisite to understanding, there may be a tendency to list the specific types of performance for both under any objective concerned with understanding. Although this practice might appear sensible at first glance, it should generally be avoided. If it were carried to an extreme, for example, the most complex objective would have to include all of the specific types of performance listed under all of the other objectives. It is much better to define each instructional objective with the specific types of performance that are unique to that particular objective. When we define *knowledge of principles* and *understanding of principles* separately, for example, we are then able to identify those students who can demonstrate achievement of the knowledge outcomes but not those of understanding. This enhances the diagnostic value of the objectives for both teaching and testing.

Revising the General Objectives As Needed

During the process of defining the general instructional objectives, it may be necessary to modify the original list. In identifying the specific learning outcomes for the objectives, you may realize that some of them are too general and need to be subdivided. An objective on *problem solving* in arithmetic, for example, might better express instructional intent if it is broken down into *computational skill* and *solving story problems.* In defining other objectives, you might note that the specific learning outcomes overlap to such a degree that it is desirable to combine two statements into a single objective. Thus, *applies scientific procedures* and *plans simple experiments* might best be combined into a single objective like *uses the scientific method effectively.* Because instructional objectives can be stated in many different ways and at various levels of generality, there is considerable flexibility in the formulation of the statements. The listing of the specific learning outcomes thus provides a good opportunity for evaluating the original list of instructional objectives and for revising them as necessary. The ultimate aim, of course, is to derive a final list of general objectives and specific learning outcomes that most clearly indicates your instructional intent.

Summary of Steps for Defining Instructional Objectives

In general summary, the procedure for defining instructional objectives in terms of student performance includes the following steps:

1. State the general instructional objectives as *expected learning outcomes.*
2. Place under each general instructional objective a list of specific learning outcomes that describes the *terminal performance* students are to demonstrate when they have achieved the *objective.*
   a. Begin each specific learning outcome with a *verb* that specifies definite *observable performance* and conveys *instructional intent.*
   b. List a *representative sample* of specific learning outcomes under each objective to adequately describe the performance of students who have achieved the objective.
   c. Add a third level of specificity to the list of outcomes, or illustrate with sample test items, if needed.
   d. Keep the specific learning outcomes relatively free of course content so that the list can be used with different units of study.
   e. Be certain that each specific learning outcome is *relevant* to the objective it describes.
3. When defining the general instructional objectives in terms of specific learning outcomes, revise and refine the original list of objectives as needed.
4. Be careful not to omit complex objectives (e.g., critical thinking) simply because they are difficult to define in terms of specific learning outcomes.
5. Consult reference materials for help in identifying the specific types of performance that are most appropriate for defining the complex objectives.

Chapter 4

Preparing an Appropriate Set
of Instructional Objectives

Now that you know how to state objectives so that they clearly convey the intended outcomes of instruction, let's take a look at the total process of preparing a list of objectives for a given course or instructional unit. How do you get started? What are some of the considerations? Where can you get ideas for objectives? How do you select and review objectives for the final list? In other words, how do you put it all together so that you end up with an appropriate list for the planned instruction.

Start with a Simple Framework

One way to get started without too much confusion is to begin with a framework that is familiar to most teachers. That is, to use the categories of *knowledge, understanding,* and *application,* and then to add the skills and affective outcomes as appropriate. Although we can expect any list of learning outcomes to vary from one content area to another and from one instructional level to another, there are some types of outcomes that are common to many instructional areas (see Box 1). Using these as a starting point, the list later can be modified and expanded as needed.

A more comprehensive and systematic list of learning outcomes is presented in a taxonomy of educational objectives that attempts to classify all possible outcomes of instruction. The three major categories, each with its own classification system, are as follows:

Cognitive: Outcomes involving intellectual tasks.
Affective: Outcomes involving feelings and emotions.
Psychomotor: Outcomes concerned with performance skills.

1. TYPES OF LEARNING OUTCOMES COMMON TO MANY AREAS AND LEVELS OF INSTRUCTION	
KNOWLEDGE of (Simple recalling of)	terms facts
UNDERSTANDING of (Grasping the Meaning of)	symbols rules concepts
APPLICATION of (Using in a Situation)	principles procedures
SKILL in	reading writing computing listening speaking problem solving thinking laboratory procedures psychomotor activity
ATTITUDE toward	subject activities self others institutions vocations

These three taxonomy categories are described in Chapter 5, and illustrative objectives and relevant action verbs are presented for each category. Reviewing the tables in Chapter 5 will make clear the large variety of learning outcomes that might be considered when preparing a list of instructional objectives. It is best to start with a simple framework and then review the taxonomy categories to expand the list and prevent any serious omissions in the final set of objectives.

Don't Neglect Complex Learning Outcomes

In any area of instruction there are some relatively simple learning outcomes that are easy to define and measure. There are also some complex learning outcomes for which definition and measurement are extremely difficult. The following paired examples, taken from different areas of instruction, illustrate the two extremes.

Simple Outcomes	Complex Outcomes
Computational skill	Mathematical reasoning
Rules of capitalization	Writing skill
Knowledge of facts	Critical thinking skills
Use of laboratory equipment	Use of the scientific method
Knowledge of vocabulary	Reading comprehension

Even a cursory comparison of these lists indicates the greater relative educational importance of the complex outcomes. All too frequently however, the *simple* outcomes are the ones that are likely to be emphasized because they are so much easier to define and measure.

The problems of definition and measurement become even greater when we consider learning outcomes in the affective area. Most educators would agree to the importance of students' developing greater creativity, positive self-concepts, and attitudes of social concern. Outcomes of this type, however, are least amenable to definition, and their evaluation depends largely on rather crude techniques (e.g., observation and self-report methods). Unless special attention is given to this area, it is likely to be under-emphasized or not included at all in a list of intended learning outcomes.

In addition to the difficulty of defining and measuring complex learning outcomes in the cognitive and affective domains, there is another reason why such outcomes are likely to be neglected. They develop so much more slowly than simple knowledge and skill outcomes. Some of them develop so slowly (e.g., critical thinking skills) that changes over a short period are difficult to detect. Thus, many of the important outcomes of instruction are not only complex but they are long-term outcomes that do not fit the simple teach-and-test model that is appropriate for short-term outcomes.

Rather than neglecting complex learning outcomes simply because they are difficult to define and measure, it is better to *identify all important intended outcomes, define them as clearly as possible, and measure each one as adequately as available measurement techniques will permit.* If important learning outcomes are neglected when measuring student performance, they are also likely to be neglected by the students. After all, students tend to concentrate on those things that count.

Reviewing the taxonomy categories in Chapter 5, as suggested earlier, will direct attention to the numerous types of complex learning outcomes that might be considered for use in your instructional area.

Don't Overlook Multiple-Course Objectives

Some learning outcomes are the shared responsibility of many teachers. With the increased emphasis on basic skills, for example, all of the teachers in the school may be considered teachers of basic skills. Similarly, if a school is emphasizing a particular outcome (e.g., critical thinking), then all of the teachers may be expected to give some emphasis to that intended outcome. With the increased use of computers in the classroom, all teachers may be required to teach students how to use computers in their particular subject. The following areas illustrate the broad range of categories that need to be considered when identifying multiple-course objectives.

Communication skills	Problem-solving skills
Computer skills	Social skills
Library skills	Study skills
Measuring skills	Thinking skills

Whether objectives in areas such as these are the shared responsibility of many teachers depends on the grade level of the instruction and the philosophy of the school. With the increased use of minimum competency testing in the schools, however, we can expect a greater sharing of responsibility for student learning; creating a greater need for attention to multiple-course objectives.

Prepare Instructional Objectives Cooperatively

It is desirable to have teachers prepare lists of instructional objectives cooperatively, wherever possible. This might involve teachers at the same grade level or in the same department working together, or it might involve committees of teachers representing all grade levels and all departments in the school. The cooperative development of objectives will ease the burden because the work can be divided up among the teachers. In addition, this procedure provides greater assurance that (1) teachers of the same course are emphasizing the same learning outcomes, (2) the sequence of instructional objectives from one grade level to the next or one course to the next is appropriate, (3) there is a minimum of overlap in single-course objectives (e.g., knowledge of facts), and (4) proper attention is given to multiple-course objectives in each teacher's lists.

Because many schools are now using microcomputers to store objectives and relevant test items, it is even more important that instructional objectives be developed cooperatively. These pools of objectives and test items are likely to be more complete and useful when all teachers have participated in their preparation.

When a group of teachers is cooperatively preparing lists of instructional objectives, it may be desirable to provide descriptions of the types of student responses encompassed by commonly used action verbs. This will provide for standard usage of terms and greater uniformity in the statement of objectives. A sample test task may also be used to further clarify the type of student response expected. A simple format, such as that in Table I, might be used.

TABLE I. Illustrations of How to Clarify Expected Student Responses
For Selected Action Verbs[1]

Action Verb	Types of Response	Sample Test Task
Identify*	Point to, touch, mark, encircle, match, pickup.	"Put an X under the right triangle."
Name*	Supply verbal label (orally or in writing).	"What is this type of angle called?"
Distinguish between	Identify as separate or different by marking, separating into classes, or selecting out a common kind.	"Which of the following statements are *facts* (encircle F) and which are opinions (encircle O)?"
Define	Supply a verbal description (orally or in writing) that gives the precise meaning or essential qualities.	"Define each of the following terms."
Describe*	Supply a verbal account (orally or in writing) that gives the essential categories, properties, and relationships.	"Describe a procedure for measuring relative humidity in the atmosphere."
Classify	Place into groups having common characteristics; assign to a particular category.	"Write the name of the type of pronoun used in each of the following sentences."
Order*	List in order, place in sequence, arrange, rearrange.	"Arrange the following historical events in chronological order."
Construct*	Draw, make, design, assemble, prepare, build.	"Draw a bar graph using the following data."
Demonstrate*	Perform a set of procedures with, or without, a verbal explanation.	"Set up the laboratory equipment for this experiment."

*Sullivan states that these six action verbs (and their synonyms) encompass nearly all cognitive learning outcomes in the school. See H. J. Sullivan, "Objectives, Evaluation, and Improved Learner Achievements," in *Instructional Objectives,* AERA Monograph Series on Curriculum Evaluation, No. 3, Chicago: Rand McNally, 1969.

[1] Reprinted from N. E. Gronlund, *Measurement and Evaluation in Teaching,* 5th ed., New York: Macmillan, 1985. Used by permission.

Getting Ideas for Instructional Objectives

As noted earlier, the *Taxonomy of Educational Objectives* provides a broad view of the variety of learning outcomes that might be considered when preparing instructional objectives. In addition to the use of this resource, you might also get ideas by consulting lists of instructional objectives developed by others and by reviewing your own teaching materials and methods.

1. Consulting Lists of Objectives Developed by Others. Reviewing lists of instructional objectives developed by others can also be useful in suggesting learning outcomes to consider and in noting the different ways objectives may be organized for a particular instructional area. Consulting other lists is usually most helpful after you have developed a tentative list of your own. At that point, you are less likely to uncritically adopt objectives that may be inappropriate for your instructional situation. Moreover, a review of other lists of objectives enables you to check the comprehensiveness of your list and to obtain ideas for improving it.

There are a number of sources for obtaining lists of instructional objectives. Most books on methods of teaching discuss objectives, present illustrative lists, and contain references that will help you locate others. The yearbooks and the special reports issued by the National Council of Teachers of English, the National Council of Teachers of Mathematics, the National Council for the Social Studies, and the National Science Teachers Association also contain suggested lists of objectives from time to time. In addition, books concerned with testing and evaluation in a particular instructional area will commonly devote some attention to instructional objectives.

An especially helpful guide for locating objectives in a specific instructional area is the *Encyclopedia of Educational Research.* It summarizes educational research on various topics, including research concerned with particular instructional areas. To use the *Encyclopedia of Educational Research,* simply consult the section on the teaching of the particular subject in which you are interested. There you will typically find references to statements of instructional objectives.

Another source of ideas for instructional objectives is found in the curriculum guides prepared on the state and local levels. Although some guides simply list the content to be covered at each grade level, others include lists of instructional objectives. Some college libraries keep files of such curriculum guides for teachers in training. Many of the larger schools may, on request, send you a copy of their curriculum guide. In obtaining ideas for instructional objectives from these various sources, you are likely to encounter two major problems. First, the lists of objectives in a given instructional area will show considerable variation in terms of emphasis and coverage. Thus, some lists will contain objectives that are not relevant to your situation, whereas others will neglect areas you consider important. Second, the lists will vary considerably in how the objectives are stated. Some will be stated in very general terms only, and others will be specified in great detail. Some will be stated in terms of the teacher, and others will be stated in terms of the student. Some will be stated as performance objectives, and others will be stated in nonperformance terms. This wide variation in content and form of statement simply means that care must be taken in adapting any list of objectives for your use. It also highlights the importance of developing a tentative list before consulting outside sources. If you have a reasonably clear idea of what the intended learning outcomes should be for your instructional area, you are less apt to be confused or undesirably influenced by the various lists of objectives. In the final analysis, your list of instructional objectives should, of course, be designed to fit your particular instructional situation.

2. Examining Your Own Teaching Materials and Methods. If you are presently teaching, your instructional procedures offer another source of ideas because instructional objectives are implicit in the materials and methods used in the classroom. Although the ideal situation would be to select teaching materials and teaching methods after identifying the expected learning outcomes, this procedure is not always possible. The textbook and other teaching materials may have been assigned by superiors. Likewise, your present teaching methods may have been determined partly by the required teaching materials and partly by past experience. In some cases, you may simply not have been exposed to this procedure for stating instructional objectives as learning outcomes until you had been teaching for some time. In any event, the materials and methods presently being used in your instruction provide another guide to the identification of instructional objectives. Your task is simply to make the implicit objectives explicit.

First, go through the subject matter included in your instruction, topic by topic, and ask yourself, "Why is this being taught?" Although the question may be difficult to answer at times, this procedure will help make explicit those objectives that are directly related to the nature of the subject matter.

Next, examine your other teaching materials in a similar manner. In using a world map, for instance, are you attempting to increase the students knowledge of specific facts, their understanding of geographic principles, their ability to interpret maps—or all three? Recalling how the map is used will help you identify the instructional objectives being sought.

Then examine your teaching methods. Some instructional objectives are direct outcomes of the methods used. Having students prepare written reports based on library work, for example, may imply that you value such outcomes as ability to locate information, ability to do independent work, and ability to write effectively. Similarly, having students participate in group activities may imply that you value outcomes concerned with interests, attitudes, or certain aspects of social adjustment.

In examining your present instructional procedures for implied objectives, you will most likely find some aspects of content and method that should be changed. This recognition of the need for change is a common by-product of the examination process. When examined in the light of expected learning outcomes, some aspects of instruction appear hard to justify. If you are an English teacher who places high value on appreciation of poetry, for example, you might begin to question whether the students' memorization of poems is actually contributing to the attainment of this objective. Similarly, if you are a teacher of biology who requires students to spend endless hours drawing what they see through the microscope, you might begin to wonder if other procedures might not contribute more directly to their laboratory skills. Or if you are a social studies teacher, you might come to realize that additional work must be added to the course if critical thinking is to be developed. Whatever your instructional area, the process of reviewing your teaching methods and materials in order to identify the objectives implicit in their use is likely to have the desirable effect of bringing your instructional procedures and instructional objectives into closer alignment.

Considerations in Reviewing and Selecting Objectives

It is usually possible to identify many more objectives than can be achieved in a particular course or instructional unit. Thus, you must be selective when you compile the final list. The following questions will serve as criteria for appraising the adequacy of the objectives to be included.

1. Do the Objectives Indicate Learning Outcomes That Are Appropriate to the Instructional Area? This question has no simple answers, but it is one that has to be considered. Here we must turn to the recommendations of experts in the curriculum area in which you plan to teach. What learning outcomes do they consider to be most important? There will not be complete agreement here, but a review of their recommendations will help in identifying the objectives that have the greatest support of curriculum specialists. This review will prevent any serious omissions and will provide greater assurance that your final list of objectives is in harmony with the most recent developments in the area.

2. Do the Objectives Represent All Logical Learning Outcomes of the Instructional Area? Here we are concerned with the comprehensiveness and representativeness of the list of objectives. For example, are objectives included from all three areas of the taxonomy—cognitive, affective, and psychomotor? Is there a proper balance among the three areas and within each area? There is a common tendency among teachers in areas where intellectual skills are dominant to overemphasize knowledge of specific facts and to neglect complex intellectual outcomes, attitudes, interests, and skills. On the other hand, teachers in areas where performance skills are dominant (art, music, physical education) frequently neglect the cognitive outcomes to be achieved. A more adequate balance of learning outcomes can be attained by reviewing the categories in the *Taxonomy of Educational Objectives* and by checking these categories against the recommendations of curriculum experts.

3. Are the Objectives Attainable by These Particular Students? To answer this question, we need to consider the ability to the students and their cultural background. Is the student group gifted, average, or of low ability? Or do we have a heterogeneous group, ranging from gifted to nearly mentally retarded? Are some or all of the students from culturally disadvantaged homes? The nature of the student group and their readiness for particular learning experiences are important considerations in formulating and selecting objectives. Closely related concerns are the time allowed for the instruction and the facilities and teaching materials available. The development of thinking skills and changes in attitude, for example, are extremely time-consuming because they depend on the cumulative effect of a long series of learning experiences. Similarly, some outcomes (e.g., skill in the scientific method) may require special laboratory facilities and special teaching materials. We are not suggesting here that otherwise desirable objectives be discarded, but simply that they may need to be modified to fit the student group and the instructional conditions under which they are to be achieved.

4. Are the Objectives in Harmony with the Philosophy of the School in Which the Instruction Is to Be Given? This would be an easy criterion to apply if each school had a clear statement of philosophy or a list of educational objectives to serve as a guide. Unfortunately, most schools do not. Thus, you must infer which outcomes are most valued in a particular school. If there appears to be an emphasis on independent work, self-discipline, freedom to explore new areas, and the democratic planning of activities, for example, these emphases should be reflected in the final list of instructional objectives. Similarly, if every teacher is expected to stress effective oral and written communication, critical thinking, and the relation of his or her subject to the other subjects in the school curriculum, a broader range of instructional objectives than might otherwise be the case will need to be included. In short, your instructional objectives should be in harmony with the stated or implicit objectives of the total school program.

5. Are the Objectives in Harmony with Basic Principles of Learning? As we indicated earlier, our instructional objectives should be stated as desired learning outcomes. Thus, it is legitimate to ask to what extent our objectives are in harmony with what is known about the principles of learning. Some of the basic factors that should be considered are the following:

1. *Readiness.* Are the students mature enough to attain these particular objectives? Do the students have the necessary experiences and educational background to proceed successfully? Is there another level at which some of the objectives might be attained more readily?
2. *Motivation.* Do these particular objectives reflect the needs and interests of the students? Can they be restated or modified to be more closely related to the

students' concerns? Is there another stage of development where these objectives would more closely fit the students' emerging interest?

3. *Retention.* Do these particular objectives reflect learning outcomes that tend to be retained longest (e.g., understanding, application. etc.)? Are there other objectives that might be more lasting and that should be included?

4. *Transfer value.* Do these particular objectives reflect learning outcomes that are widely applicable to new situations? Do the objectives include methods of study and modes of thinking that are most likely to contribute to future learning in the area?

These questions are not always easily answered, but they highlight the importance of considering the learning process when you formulate and select instructional objectives. Most general textbooks on educational psychology will provide extended discussions of the basic learning principles. It is sufficient to point out here that the more complex learning outcomes tend to be retained longer and to have greater transfer value. When they are appropriate to the developmental level of the learner, the more complex outcomes also have the greatest potential for arousing and maintaining student interest.

To summarize, the preparation of a list of instructional objectives for a particular course or instructional unit requires the careful selection of those objectives that are most pertinent to the instructional area. Ideas for appropriate objectives can be obtained from the *Taxonomy of Educational Objectives,* as well as from lists included in books, journal articles, and curriculum guides of other schools. To identify those objectives that are implicit in your present instruction, you should analyze the teaching methods and materials that you are currently using. Criteria for selecting instructional objectives for the final list include appropriateness, representativeness, attainability, relationship to the total school program, and relationship to the basic principles of learning.

Chapter 5

Using the Taxonomy of Educational Objectives

One of the most helpful guides in identifying and defining instructional objectives is the *Taxonomy of Educational Objectives,* developed by committees under the direction of Bloom (1956) and Krathwohl (1964). The taxonomy provides a classification of educational objectives that is analogous to the classification scheme used for plants and animals. It consists of a set of general and specific categories that encompass all possible learning outcomes that might be expected from instruction. The classification system was developed by psychologists, teachers, and test experts for use in curriculum development, teaching, and testing. Because the system is based on the assumption that learning outcomes can be best described in terms of changes in student performance, it is especially useful to teachers who are attempting to state their instructional objectives in performance terms.

The taxonomy is divided into three main parts: (1) the cognitive domain, (2) the affective domain, and (3) the psychomotor domain. The cognitive domain includes those objectives that emphasize intellectual outcomes, such as knowledge, understanding, and thinking skills. The affective domain includes those objectives that emphasize feeling and emotion, such as interests, attitudes, appreciation, and methods of adjustment. The psychomotor domain includes those objectives that emphasize motor skills, such as handwriting, typing, swimming, and operating machinery. A complete classification system was developed for the cognitive and affective domains by the Bloom and Krathwohl committees, but the preparation of the psychomotor domain was never completed. In recent years, however, at least two major classification systems for the psychomotor domain have been prepared, neither one by the original taxonomy developers. We shall present one of these psychomotor systems for illustrative purposes.

The Cognitive and Affective Domains

The cognitive and affective domains have the most highly developed and detailed classification systems. The categories and subcategories in each of these domains are arranged in hierarchical order, from the simplest outcomes to the most complex. The cognitive domain, for example, starts with simple knowledge outcomes and then proceeds through the increasingly complex levels of comprehension, application, analysis, synthesis, and evaluation. Each category is assumed to include the behavior at the lower levels. Thus comprehension includes the behavior at the knowledge level; application includes that at both the knowledge and comprehension levels, and so on. The affective domain follows a similar hierarchical pattern, ranging from the simple receiving of stimuli to the development of a value system that characterizes an individual's life style.

On following pages, In tables II and IV, are brief descriptions of each of the major categories in the cognitive and affective domains. Accompanying Tables (III and V) also present examples of objectives and illustrative verbs for stating the specific learning outcomes for each of the categories. These examples should help clarify the meaning of each category and suggest types of learning outcomes to consider when identifying and defining instructional objectives. The illustrative objectives are not exhaustive, of course, but a reveiw of them should stimulate you to think of a broader range of objectives for your particular area of instruction.

The list of verbs for each taxonomy category is only a sample of some of the more relevant action verbs. It must also be kept in mind that frequently the same term may be appropriately used at several levels. The term *identifies,* for example, is appropriate in each of the following cases:

Knowledge:	Identifies the correct definition of the term.
Understanding:	Identifies examples of the principle.
Application:	Identifies proper grammar usage.
Analysis:	Identifies the parts of a sentence.

Despite this considerable overlap in the use of terms, there are some action verbs that are more directly relevant to one taxonomy category than to another. Those listed in the tables are merely suggestive; but they can assist in selecting the terms that most clearly convey the instructional intent of a given objective. More comprehensive lists of action verbs for stating specific learning are presented in Appendix B.

If you would like more elaborate and detailed treatments of the cognitive and affective domains, see the handbooks by Bloom (1956) and Krathwohl (1964) in the list of references in Appendix C. Both books provide extensive descriptions of the major and minor categories, with numerous illustrative objectives and test items.

The Psychomotor Domain

The psychomotor domain is concerned with motor skills. Although this domain includes some learning outcomes that are common to most subjects (writing, speaking, laboratory skills), it receives major emphasis in commercial subjects, health sciences, home economics, industrial education, physical education, art, and music. Performance skills play a prominent role in the instructional objectives in these areas.

The classification system for the psychomotor domain that is shown in Table VI is one developed by Simpson (1972). It was selected for use because the categories seem appropriate for classifying a wide variety of different type motor skills. The major categories, ranging from perception (the lowest level) to origination (the highest level), have a hierarchical arrangement similar to that in the cognitive and affective domains. As with the other two domains, illustrative objectives and relevant action verbs are presented for each category (see Tabe VII), to further clarify the various performance levels and to suggest types of learning outcomes to consider.

A taxonomy in the psychomotor domain has also been developed by Harrow (1972). Her taxonomy seems to be especially well adapted to the area of physical education, but may prove useful in other areas as well.

Instructional objectives in the psychomotor domain typically include concomitant cognitive and affective elements, but the demonstration of a motor skill is the dominant characteristic of the student's response. This over-lapping of behavior from the different domains is, of course, not limited to performance skills. Learning outcomes in the cognitive area have some affective elements, and outcomes in the affective area have some cognitive components. The three domains of the taxonomy provide a useful classification system, but they simply represent particular emphases in stating objectives and not mutually exclusive divisions.

In summary, the *Taxonomy of Educational Objectives* provides a three-domain scheme (cognitive, affective, and psychomotor) for classifying all possible instructional objectives. Each domain is subdivided into a series of categories that are arranged in hierarchical order—from simple to complex. A review of these categories and the illustrative objectives and action verbs accompanying them (Tables II to VII) should aid in (1) identifying objectives for a particular instructional unit, (2) stating objectives at the proper level of generality, (3) defining objectives in the most relevant terms, (4) checking on the comprehensiveness of a list of objectives, and (5) communicating with others concerning the nature and level of learning outcomes included in a list of objectives.

As useful as the taxonomy may be, don't become a slave to the system of classification. Some objectives will include elements of all three taxonomy domains. Such objectives should not be discarded simply because they are difficult to classify. Use the taxonomy only as a guide.

TABLE II. Major Categories in the Cognitive Domain of the Taxonomy of
Educational Objectives (Bloom, 1956)

Descriptions of the Major Categories in the Cognitive Domain

1. **Knowledge.** Knowledge is defined as the remembering of previously learned material. This may involve the recall of a wide range of material, from specific facts to complete theories, but all that is required is the bringing to mind of the appropriate information. Knowledge represents the lowest level of learning outcomes in the cognitive domain.

2. **Comprehension.** Comprehension is defined as the ability to grasp the meaning of material. This may be shown by translating material from one form to another (words to numbers), by interpreting material (explaining or summarizing), and by estimating future trends (predicting consequences or effects). These learning outcomes go one step beyond the simple remembering of material, and represent the lowest level of understanding.

3. **Application.** Application refers to the ability to use learned material in new and concrete situations. This may include the application of such things as rules, methods, concepts, principles, laws, and theories. Learning outcomes in this area require a higher level of understanding than those under comprehension.

4. **Analysis.** Analysis refers to the ability to break down material into its component parts so that its organizational structure may be understood. This may include the identification of the parts, analysis of the relationships between parts, and recognition of the organizational principles involved. Learning outcomes here represent a higher intellectual level than comprehension and application because they require an understanding of both the content and the structural form of the material.

5. **Synthesis.** Synthesis refers to the ability to put parts together to form a new whole. This may involve the production of a unique communication (theme or speech), a plan of operations (research proposal), or a set of abstract relations (scheme for classifying information). Learning outcomes in this area stress creative behaviors, with major emphasis on the formulation of *new* patterns of structures.

6. **Evaluation.** Evaluation is concerned with the ability to judge the value of material (statement, novel, poem, research report) for a given purpose. The judgments are to be based on definite criteria. These may be internal criteria (organization) or external criteria (relevance to the purpose) and the student may determine the criteria or be given them. Learning outcomes in this area are highest in the cognitive hierarchy because they contain elements of all of the other categories, plus conscious value judgments based on clearly defined criteria.

TABLE III. Examples of General Instructional Objections and Clarifying Verbs
for the Cognitive Domain of the Taxonomy

Illustrative General Instructional Objectives	*Illustrative Verbs for Stating Specific Learning Outcomes*
Knows common terms Knows specific facts Knows methods and procedures Knows basic concepts Knows principles	Defines, describes, identifies, labels, lists, matches, names, outlines, reproduces, selects, states
Understands facts and principles Interprets verbal material Interprets charts and graphs Translates verbal material to mathematical formulas Estimates future consequences implied in data Justifies methods and procedures	Converts, defends, distinguishes, estimates, explains, extends, generalizes, gives examples, infers, paraphrases, predicts, rewrites, summarizes
Applies concepts and principles to new situations Applies laws and theories to practical situations Solves mathematical problems Constructs charts and graphs Demonstrates correct usage of a method or procedure	Changes, computes, demonstrates, discovers, manipulates, modifies, operates, predicts, prepares, produces, relates, shows, solves, uses
Recognizes unstated assumptions Recognizes logical fallacies in reasoning Distinguishes between facts and inferences Evaluates the relevancy of data Analyzes the organizational structure of a work (art, music, writing)	Breaks down, diagrams, differentiates, discriminates, distinguishes, identifies, illustrates, infers, outlines, points out, relates, selects, separates, subdivides
Writes a well organized theme Gives a well organized speech Writes a creative short story (or poem, or music) Proposes a plan for an experiment Integrates learning from different areas into a plan for solving a problem Formulates a new scheme for classifying objects (or events, or ideas)	Categorizes, combines, compiles, composes, creates, devises, designs, explains, generates, modifies, organizes, plans, rearranges, reconstructs, relates, reorganizes, revises, rewrites, summarizes, tells, writes
Judges the logical consistency of written material Judges the adequacy with which conclusions are supported by data Judges the value of a work (art, music, writing) by use of internal criteria Judges the value of a work (art, music, writing) by use of external standards of excellence	Appraises, compares, concludes, contrasts, criticizes, describes, discriminates, explains, justifies, interprets, relates, summarizes, supports

TABLE IV. Major Categories in the Affective Domain of the Taxonomy of
Educational Objectives (Krathwohl, 1964)

Descriptions of the Major Categories in the Affective Domain

1. **Receiving.** Receiving refers to the student's willingness to attend to particular phenomena or stimuli (classroom activities, textbook, music, etc.). From a teaching standpoint, it is concerned with getting, holding, and directing the student's attention. Learning outcomes in this area range from the simple awareness that a thing exists to selective attention on the part of the learner. Receiving represents the lowest level of learning outcomes in the affective domain.

2. **Responding.** Responding refers to active participation on the part of the student. At this level he or she not only attends to a particular phenomenon but also reacts to it in some way. Learning outcomes in this area may emphasize acquiescence in responding (reads assigned material), willingness to respond (voluntarily reads beyond assignment), or satisfaction in responding (reads for pleasure or enjoyment). The higher levels of this category include those instructional objectives that are commonly classified under "interests"; that is, those that stress the seeking out and enjoyment of particular activities.

3. **Valuing.** Valuing is concerned with the worth or value a student attaches to a particular object, phenomenon, or behavior. This ranges in degree from the more simple acceptance of a value (desires to improve group skills) to the more complex level of commitment (assumes responsibility for the effective functioning of the group). Valuing is based on the internalization of a set of specified values, but clues to these values are expressed in the student's overt behavior. Learning outcomes in this area are concerned with behavior that is consistent and stable enough to make the value clearly identifiable. Instructional objectives that are commonly classified under "attitudes" and "appreciation" would fall into this category.

4. **Organization.** Organization is concerned with bringing together different values, resolving conflicts between them, and beginning the building of an internally consistent value system. Thus the emphasis is on comparing, relating, and synthesizing values. Learning outcomes may be concerned with the conceptualization of a value (recognizes the responsibility of each individual for improving human relations) or with the organization of a value system (develops a vocational plan that satisfies his or her need for both economic security and social service). Instructional objectives relating to the development of a philosophy of life would fall into this category.

5. **Characterization by a Value or Value Complex.** At this level of the affective domain the individual has a value system that has controlled his or her behavior for a sufficiently long time for him or her to have developed a characteristic "life-style." Thus the behavior is pervasive, consistent, and predictable. Learning outcomes at this level cover a broad range of activities, but the major emphasis is on the fact that the behavior is typical or characteristic of the student. Instructional objectives that are concerned with the student's general patterns of adjustment (personal, social, emotional) would be appropriate here.

TABLE V. Examples of General Instructional Objectives and Clarifying Verbs for the Affective Domain of the Taxonomy

Illustrative General Instructional Objectives	*Illustrative Verbs for Stating Specific Learning Outcomes*
Listens attentively Shows awareness of the importance of learning Shows sensitivity to human needs and social problems Accepts differences of race and culture Attends closely to the classroom activities	Asks, chooses, describes, follows, gives, holds, identifies, locates, names, points to, selects, sits erect, replies, uses
Completes assigned homework Obeys school rules Participates in class discussion Completes laboratory work Volunteers for special tasks Shows interest in subject Enjoys helping others	Answers, assists, complies, conforms, discusses, greets, helps, labels, performs, practices, presents, reads, recites, reports, selects, tells, writes
Demonstrates belief in the democratic process Appreciates good literature (art or music) Appreciates the role of science (or other subjects) in everyday life Shows concern for the welfare of others Demonstrates problem-solving attitude Demonstrates commitment to social improvement	Completes, describes, differentiates, explains, follows, forms, initiates, invites, joins, justifies, proposes, reads, reports, selects, shares, studies, works
Recognizes the need for balance between freedom and responsibility in a democracy Recognizes the role of systematic planning in solving problems Accepts responsibility for his or her own behavior Understands and accepts his or her own strengths and limitations Formulates a life plan in harmony with his or her abilities, interests, and beliefs	Adheres, alters, arranges, combines, compares, completes, defends, explains, generalizes, identifies, integrates, modifies, orders, organizes, prepares, relates, synthesizes
Displays safety consciousness Demonstrates self-reliance working independently Practices cooperation in group activities Uses objective approach in problem solving Demonstrates industry, punctuality and self-discipline Maintains good health habits	Acts, discriminates, displays, influences, listens, modifies, performs, practices, proposes, qualifies, questions, revises, serves, solves, uses, verifies

TABLE VI. A Classification of Educational Objectives in the
Psychomotor Domain (Simpson, 1972)

Description of the Major Categories in the Psychomotor Domain

1. **Perception.** The first level is concerned with the use of the sense organs to obtain cues that guide motor activity. This category ranges from sensory stimulation (awareness of a stimulus), through cue selection (selecting task-relevant cues), to translation (relating cue perception to action in a performance).

2. **Set.** Set refers to readiness to take a particular type of action. This category includes mental set (mental readiness to act), physical set (physical readiness to act), and emotional set (willingness to act). Perception of cues serves as an important prerequisite for this level.

3. **Guided Response.** Guided response is concerned with the early stages in learning a complex skill. It includes imitation (repeating an act demonstrated by the instructor) and trial and error (using a multiple-response approach to identify an appropriate response). Adequacy of performance is judged by an instructor or by a suitable set of criteria.

4. **Mechanism.** Mechanism is concerned with performance acts where the learned responses have become habitual and the movements can be performed with some confidence and proficiency. Learning outcomes at this level are concerned with performance skills of various types, but the movement patterns are less complex than at the next higher level.

5. **Complex Overt Response.** Complex Overt Response is concerned with the skillful performance of motor acts that involve complex movement patterns. Proficiency is indicated by a quick, smooth, accurate performance, requiring a minimum of energy. This category includes resolution of uncertainty (performs without hesitation) and automatic performance (movements are made with ease and good muscle control). Learning outcomes at this level include highly coordinated motor activities.

6. **Adaptation.** Adaptation is concerned with skills that are so well developed that the individual can modify movement patterns to fit special requirements or to meet a problem situation.

7. **Origination.** Origination refers to the creating of new movement patterns to fit a particular situation or specific problem. Learning outcomes at this level emphasize creativity based upon highly developed skills

TABLE VII. Examples of General Instructional Objectives
and Clarifying Verbs for the Psychomotor Domain

Illustrative General Instructional Objectives	*Illustrative Verbs for Stating Specific Learning Outcomes*
Recognizes malfunction by sound of machine Relates taste of food to need for seasoning Relates music to a particular dance step	Chooses, describes, detects, differentiates, distinguishes, identifies, isolates, relates, selects, separates
Knows sequence of steps in varnishing wood Demonstrates proper bodily stance for batting a ball Shows desire to type efficiently	Begins, displays, explains, moves, proceeds, reacts, responds, shows, starts, volunteers
Performs a golf swing as demonstrated Applies first-aid bandage as demonstrated Determines best sequence for preparing a meal	Assembles, builds, calibrates, constructs, dismantles, displays, dissects, fastens, fixes, grinds, heats, manipulates, measures, mends mixes, organizes, sketches, works
Writes smoothly and legibly Sets up laboratory equipment Operates a slide projector Demonstrates a simple dance step	(Same list as for Guided Response)
Operates a power saw skillfully Demonstrates correct form in swimming Demonstrates skill in driving an automobile Performs skillfully on the violin Repairs electronic equipment quickly and accurately	(Same list as for Guided Response)
Adjusts tennis play to counteract opponent's style Modifies swimming strokes to fit the roughness of the water	Adapts, alters, changes, rearranges, reorganizes, revises, varies
Creates a dance step Creates a musical composition Designs a new dress style	Arranges, combines, composes, constructs, designs, originates

Chapter 6

Relating Objectives to Classroom Instruction

The final list of instructional objectives usually contains some learning outcomes that are considered essential for all students to achieve and others that allow for varying degrees of individual development. In arithmetic, for example, we might expect all students to know the multiplication table, but we anticipate considerable variation in the ability of students to solve problems requiring arithmetical reasoning. Similarly, we may consider it essential for all chemistry students to know the formulas of the chemical compounds studied, but we can expect wide variation in their ability to apply scientific principles to new situations. Learning outcomes that are considered *minimum essentials* are typically low-level outcomes that can be rather easily achieved by students and that serve as prerequisites to further learning in the area. Those outcomes at the *developmental level* represent goals toward which students may show different degrees of progress but which they never fully achieve. The ability to understand, to apply, to interpret, and to think critically, for example, typically depend on an extended period of development. Their complete attainment is not expected in any given course. All we can expect to do here is to define each objective in terms of those outcomes that are appropriate to the students' learning levels and that represent reasonable degrees of progress toward the objective.

Failure to distinguish between instructional objectives that are considered minimum essentials and those that encourage maximum development has caused considerable confusion in both teaching and testing. Some teachers tend to treat all objectives as minimum essentials and to strive for mastery on the part of all students. Where this is done, the more simple learning outcomes are stressed, teaching and testing tend to focus on specific learning tasks, and an attempt is made to keep all students learning at the same level. In contrast to this approach, some teachers stress objectives at the developmental level only. They put so much emphasis on these more complex learning outcomes that they neglect the knowledge and skills that are prerequisite to a higher order of learning. To avoid these extremes, you should give consideration to both types of objectives when you prepare the list of intended learning outcomes, and you should use teaching and testing procedures that accommodate both types of outcomes.

Teaching and Testing at the "Minimum Essentials Level"

The teaching emphasis at the *minimum-essentials level* is on shaping and modifying student behavior to fit a predetermined and clearly defined minimum level of performance. The learning outcomes are generally very specific and call for simple, independent responses. In fact, the objectives are frequently stated as tasks to be performed rather than as goals to work toward. Thus, we might have statements like the following:

> Adds single-digit whole numbers.
> Identifies symbols used on weather maps.
> Defines basic terms of unit.
> Identifies parts of the microscope.

Such simple and clearly defined tasks make it possible to have a one-to-one relation between the stated objective, the teaching procedure, and the testing procedure. As illustrated in the following diagram, the specific learning outcome is stated, the specific task is directly taught, and the specific task is directly tested:

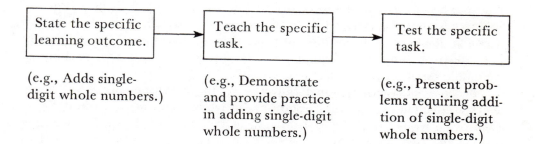

State the specific learning outcome.	Teach the specific task.	Test the specific task.
(e.g., Adds single-digit whole numbers.)	(e.g., Demonstrate and provide practice in adding single-digit whole numbers.)	(e.g., Present problems requiring addition of single-digit whole numbers.)

This is the model used in programmed learning and in teaching at the training level. This model is very useful for illustrating the direct relationship between objectives, teaching, and testing in the learning of minimum essentials; that is, in those areas of learning where the desired outcome is to make all students perform alike at a specified *minimum* level. This model is inappropriate, however, for teaching and testing at the developmental level, as we shall see shortly.

Standards of performance are most frequently specified in the learning of minimum essentials. These standards may indicate that complete or nearly complete mastery is expected. Thus, a student may be expected "to identify *all* of the parts of a microscope," "to define *eight out of ten* terms," or "to solve *90 per cent* of the computational problems." Such standards are easily specified at this level because the learning outcomes are specific, independent, and easily defined.

Although stating the standards for a minimum level of performance is a simple process, determining what the standards should be is not. On what basis do you decide that a student should be able "to define *eight out of ten* terms"? Why shouldn't the student have to define seven, nine, or all ten? There is little evidence to support particular standards of achievement in the various subjects at different grade levels. Each teacher must depend on his or her own arbitrary judgment—based on the difficulty of the material, the nature of the student group, and the learning conditions that exist. Although such standards can provide rough guidelines for determining the extent to which a minimum level of performance is being achieved, you must always keep in mind that the standards are arbitrarily set and therefore highly tentative.

Teaching and Testing at the "Developmental Level"

The teaching emphasis at the *developmental level* is on encouraging each student to progress as far as possible toward predetermined goals. The instructional objectives here are typically more general than those at the mastery level. Rather than being stated as specific tasks to be performed, each objective represents a whole class of responses. Thus, the objectives provide direction for both the teacher and the student, without being overly restrictive with regard to the nature of the instruction or the types of learning activities to be engaged in by the student. They allow for an openness and exploration in the teaching–learning process that is absent in the closely prescribed shaping and molding process characteristic of the teaching of minimum essentials.

Because each instructional objective at the developmental level represents a large class of specific responses, all we can expect to do in defining each objective is to list a reasonably adequate *sample* of the specific learning outcomes. This process was described in Chapter 3 and is illustrated as follows:

Understands Scientific Principles

1. States the principle in his or her own words.
2. Gives an example of the principle.
3. Identifies predictions that are in harmony with the principle.
4. Distinguishes between correct and incorrect applications of the principle.

The four specific learning outcomes listed under this objective help clarify what is meant by *understands scientific principles,* but these are just four of the numerous ways that *understanding* might be shown. There-fore, these four specific types of response are representative of the variety of responses that could describe the general objective. Because we are able to list only a sample of the types of performance we are interested in, these specific learning outcomes are not expected to be taught and tested on a one-to-one basis. In fact, were this method to be followed, learning would be of a rote nature, and responses could not be used as evidence of *under-standing.* For example, if we were to teach a student to "state a principle in his or her own words" and later ask the student to "state the principle in his or her own words," the student's response would represent nothing more than the *recall* of previously learned material. The same would hold true for the other three specific learning outcomes. If all intended outcomes were taught in this manner, we would be functioning at a simple recall level, and the usefulness of the sample of performance as an indication of *under-standing* would be destroyed. That is, the students would be able to demon-strate the types of performance included in the sample (in a rote manner) but would not be able to demonstrate the other types of performance also encompassed by the same instructional objective.

Teaching at the developmental level must be directed toward the general instructional objective and the total class of responses that it represents. The list of specific learning outcomes is mainly useful in providing an opera-tional definition of the general objective and in providing guidelines for test construction.

The relation of teaching and testing to the objectives at the develop-mental level is illustrated as follows.

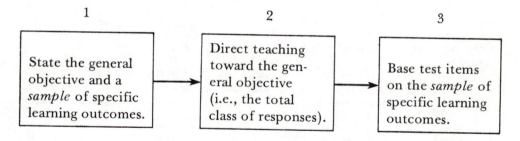

1   State the general objective and a *sample* of specific learning outcomes. → 2   Direct teaching toward the gen-eral objective (i.e., the total class of responses). → 3   Base test items on the *sample* of specific learning outcomes.

It will be noted in this diagram that the sample of specific learning out-comes that is identified in step 1 can also be used as a basis for developing the test items in step 3. In measuring such complex learning outcomes as understanding, however, the test items should go beyond what has been directly taught in step 2. In stating examples of a principle, for instance, the students should be required to state new examples (i.e., examples not discussed in class). Similarly, the application of principles should be con-cerned with new situations, and the interpretation of data should be based on data new to the students. It is only when the test items contain some novelty that we are able to go beyond the simple recall level of learning and to measure the more complex learning outcomes.

At the developmental level of learning where *maximum achievement* is the goal, useful standards of performance are extremely difficult, if not impossible, to define. Thus, it is usually necessary to describe test performance in relative terms; that is, in terms of where a given test score falls in some particular group. This may be a classroom group or, as in the case of standardized tests, a national group. In either instance, however, the test score indicates a relative level of achievement only; therefore, the nature of the group must be taken into account when you interpret the score.

A summary of some of the major differences between teaching and testing at the minimum-essentials level and at the developmental level is presented in Table VIII.

TABLE VIII.   Summary Comparison of the Relation of Objectives to Teaching and Testing at Two Different Levels of Instruction

	Minimum Essentials Level	*Developmental Level*
Teaching Emphasis	Shape and modify student behavior to fit a predetermined *minimum level of performance.*	Encourage and direct each student toward the *maximum level of development* he or she is capable of achieving.
Nature of the Objectives	Limited, specific, and completely defined tasks to be performed.	General objectives that provide direction and are defined by a *representative sample* of specific types of performance.
Relation of Teaching to the Objectives	Teaching is directed toward the specific task stated in the objective. Each *specific task* is taught on a one-to-one basis.	Teaching is directed toward the *general class of responses* that the objective represents, rather than toward the performance included in the particular sample.
Relation of Testing to the Objectives	Each specific task is tested directly on a one-to-one basis. Test items require students to demonstrate responses identical to those learned in class.	Only a *sample* of specific performance is tested for each objective. Test items require students to demonstrate previously learned responses in situations containing some novelty.
Specifying Performance Standards	Standards of minimum performance are easily specified, but they are usually set in an arbitrary manner.	Performance standards are difficult to specify. Achievement is typically reported in terms of *relative* position in some known group.

Using Objectives in Instructional Planning

The final list of objectives for a particular course or unit of work specifies the learning outcomes that are to result from the instruction. As we have noted, some of these outcomes will indicate a minimum level of performance required of all students, and some will indicate goals toward which varying degrees of progress can be expected. In any event, these objectives constitute the learning outcomes that are considered to have the greatest value for the students; therefore, they provide a sound basis for instructional planning. To be most effective, of course, the instructional objectives should be/identified and defined before other instructional plans are made. When both the methods and materials of instruction and the procedures for evaluating student progress are selected in light of the desired learning outcomes, we can expect them to be more relevant and more effective.

One way to ensure that the instructional objectives, the teaching methods, and the evaluation techniques will be in harmony is to prepare a planning chart that includes all three. The two examples in Table IX, the first at the minimum-essentials level and the second at the developmental level, illustrate the procedure for preparing a planning chart.

In using a planning chart, you must take care to prevent instruction from becoming subdivided into a series of separate teaching acts. The chart makes clear the relationship between the teaching methods, the evaluation techniques, and the desired learning outcomes, but you must not infer that each objective should be worked toward separately. *Knowledge of literary terms,* for example, may receive direct attention early in the instruction, but this is a goal to work toward throughout the course. Similarly, when students work on the *interpretation of literature,* they would also give attention to specific facts concerning the literary work, to speaking and writing skills, to an appreciation of literature, and so on. In classroom instruction, we typically work on a number of different learning outcomes at the same time. What the chart does is provide an overall plan to assure that each objective will receive the proper share of attention in the instructional process and that the methods of teaching and testing will be more relevant to the attainment of the desired learning outcomes. The chart, therefore, serves as a guide for our daily lesson planning. In these daily lesson plans, we can provide for the desired integration of the learning experiences and for their placement in proper sequence.

In summary, instructional objectives include some learning outcomes that can be considered minimum essentials and others that encourage the maximum development of the student. Most classroom instruction includes objectives of both types. A clear distinction between the types should be made because each type requires a different teaching and testing emphasis. Instructional planning is enhanced if the instructional objectives are identified first. This procedure provides greater assurance that the methods and materials of instruction and the evaluation techniques are appropriate for achieving the intended learning outcomes. An instructional planning chart, which provides a useful guide for daily lesson planning, can be used to relate these various aspects of instruction.

TABLE IX. Instructional Planning Chart

Instructional Objectives	Teaching Methods	Evaluation techniques
Knows literary terms 1. Writes textbook definitions 2. Identifies examples in a literary selection 3. Uses the terms correctly in oral and written work	Encourage students to make a "literary dictionary," and to review the definitions periodically. Point out, and ask students to point out, examples during oral reading. Give oral and written assignments requiring use of the terms.	1. Short-answer test 2. Multiple-choice test 3. Observation and evaluation of written work
Interprets literary works 1. Identifies the major and minor themes 2. States the author's purpose or message 3. Identifies the tone and mood 4. Explains why the characters behave as they do 5. Points out specific parts of the literature that support the above interpretations 6. Relates the literary work to other writings	Read a brief literary work to class. Lead off discussion with questions concerning theme, author's purpose, tone, and character development. Analyze the parts of the literary work and show how they support the general interpretations. Generalize the method of analysis and interpretation by applying it to a second work. Have students select a literary work and write a critical analysis and interpretation.	Observation during class discussions. Objective test on specific points in a literary work and on the process of literary analysis. Essay questions calling for interpretations and supporting evidence. Evaluation of student's written reports (using criteria of effective interpretation).

Chapter 7

Using Instructional Objectives in Test Preparation

An achievement test is simply a device for obtaining a *sample* of student performance. For valid results, the sample must be in harmony with both the instructional objectives and the subject matter emphasized in the instruction. A satisfactory sample is most likely to be obtained when test preparation follows a systematic procedure. The following list of steps has been found to be useful for this purpose.

1. State the general instructional objectives and define each objective in terms of the specific types of performance students are expected to demonstrate at the end of instruction. (See Chapters 2, 3, and 4.)
2. Make an outline of the content to be covered during the instruction.
3. Prepare a table of specifications that describes the nature of the test sample.
4. Construct test items that measure the sample of student performance specified in the table.

Each of these steps will be briefly described and illustrated for a unit in economics.

Defining the Objectives

Defining instructional objectives in terms of student performance serves two important purposes in test preparation: (1) It indicates the sample of specific learning outcomes that we are willing to accept as evidence that the objectives are being achieved, and (2) it specifies in precise terms the student performance that is to be measured by the test items. Because an achievement test is designed to measure a sample of student performance, it is important that the responses called forth by the test items be both relevant and representative. These conditions would probably not be met without a carefully detailed description of the intended outcomes of instruction.

Following is a brief list of instructional objectives that has been defined by a list of specific learning outcomes. This list is for illustrative purposes only and therefore is not meant to be exhaustive; the list simply demonstrates the method of stating objectives for testing purposes.

Objectives for a Unit in Economics

1. Knows basic terms.
   1.1 Relates terms that have the same meaning.
   1.2 Selects the term that best fits a particular definition.
   1.3 Identifies terms used in reference to particular economic problems.
   1.4 Uses terms correctly in describing economic problems.
2. Understands economic concepts and principles.
   2.1 Identifies examples of economic concepts and principles.
   2.2 Describes economic concepts and principles in his own words.
   2.3 Identifies the interrelationship of economic principles.
   2.4 Explains changes in economic conditions in terms of the economic concepts and principles involved.
3. Applies economic principles to new situations.
   3.1 Identifies the economic principles needed to solve a practical problem.
   3.2 Predicts the probable outcome of an action involving economic principles.
   3.3 Describes how to solve a practical economic problem in terms of the economic principles involved.
   3.4 Distinguishes between probable and improbable economic forecasts.
4. Interprets economic data.
   4.1 Differentiates between relevant and irrelevant information.
   4.2 Differentiates between facts and inferences.
   4.3 Identifies cause-effect relations in data.
   4.4 Describes the trends in data.
   4.5 Distinguishes between warranted and unwarranted conclusions drawn from data.
   4.6 States proper qualifications when describing data.

Note that the statements of specific learning outcomes listed under each general objective describe how the students are expected to react toward the subject matter in economics but do not describe the specific subject matter toward which they are to react. Therefore, the specific statements listed under *knows basic terms* describes what is meant by *knowing*—not what terms the students should know. Such statements make it possible to relate the objectives and the specific learning outcomes to various areas of content and thus to various units within the same course. As we shall see shortly, the table of specifications provides a method for relating the instructional objectives to the course content.

Outlining the Content

Because an achievement test should also adequately sample the subject matter included in the instruction, you should make an outline of the content to be covered by the test. The same content outline that is used for teaching may suffice, or a less elaborate outline may be developed as part of the test plan. The following list of topics for our illustrative unit in economics provides sufficient detail for testing purposes.

Content Outline for a Unit in Economics
(Money and Banking)

A. Forms and functions of money.
   1. Types of money.
   2. Various uses of money.
B. Operation of banks.
   1. Services provided by commercial banks.
   2. Other institutions offering banking services.
   3. Role of banks in managing the flow of money.
C. Role of the Federal Reserve System.
   1. Need for flexibility in the money supply.
   2. Nature of the Federal Reserve System.
   3. Regulatory policies influencing the money supply.
D. State regulation of banks.
   1. The state banking commission.
   2. Laws to protect the borrowers.

The amount of detail to be included in the outline of content will, of course, depend on the length of time covered by the instruction. For a two-week unit of work, you may be able to include all of the major and minor topics. In outlining the content for an entire course, however, you may have to limit the outline to the main subject headings. Restricting the length of the outline to one or two pages is usually satisfactory for test-construction purposes.

Preparing the Table of Specifications

A table of specifications is a twofold table that relates the instructional objectives to the course content. The table makes it possible to classify each test item in terms of both objectives and content. A completed table describes the number of test items needed to obtain a balanced measure of the instructional objectives and the course content emphasized in the instruction.

A sample table of specifications, based on our illustrative unit in economics, is shown in Table X. To simplify the table, we have included only the general instructional objectives and major areas of content. This procedure is typical, although more detail may be desirable in some situations.

TABLE X. Table of Specifications for a 50-Item Test on a
Unit in Economics (Money and Banking)

Content Areas	Instructional Objectives			
	1 Knows Basic Terms	2 Understands Concepts and Principles	3 Applies Principles	4 Interprets Data
A. Forms and functions of money	3	4	3	
B. Operation of banks	4	3	5	3
C. Role of the Federal Reserve System	4	6	3	2
D. State regulation of banks	4	2	4	
Total number of test items	15	15	15	5

The numbers in each cell in the table indicate the number of test items to be constructed in each area. For example, there will be a total of fifteen items that measure the objective *knows basic terms;* three of these in the content area *forms and functions of money,* four of these in the content area *operation of banks,* and so on down the column. The total number of items in each column indicates the relative emphasis to be given to each objective, and the total number of items in each row indicates the relative emphasis to be given to each area of content. Therefore, the two-way grid specifies the test sample in terms of both instructional objectives and course content.

The relative emphasis shown in the table of specifications should, of course, reflect the emphasis given during instruction. This is accomplished by assigning weights to each objective and to each content area during the construction of the table. The usual procedure is first to distribute the total number (or percentage) of test items over the objectives and content areas and then to distribute the items among the individual cells. Although a number of factors might be considered in assigning such weights, the amount of instructional time devoted to each area will usually provide a satisfactory approximation. In Table X for instance, it is assumed that the *interpretation of data* (5 test items) received only one third of the instructional emphasis given to each of the other objectives (15 test items each) and that this instruction was limited to content areas B and C. The table also indicates, by the number of items in each row, that content areas A and D received less instructional emphasis than areas B and C.

Constructing Relevant Test Items

The table of specifications describes the nature of the desired test sample and specifies what each test item should measure. The next task is to construct test items that are relevant to the instructional objectives and content areas of each cell. For example, in using Table X, let's assume that we are going to construct one of the four test items to measure the first objective (knows basic terms) in content area B (operation of banks). Our procedure would be as follows: (1) to select one of the specific learning outcomes listed under the first objective, (2) to select one of the important banking terms, and (3) to construct a test item that calls forth the specific performance indicated in the learning outcome. Our test item should clearly reflect the desired learning outcome, as follows:

Instructional Objective: 1. Knows basic terms.
Learning Outcome: 1.1 Relates terms that have the same meaning
1. Checking accounts are also called
   *A. demand deposits.
   B. time deposits.
   C. currency.
   D. credit money.

Note in the above example that the learning outcome describes the specific response we expect the students to demonstrate and that the test item presents a relevant task. Other examples at the understanding and application levels are presented below. The objectives and outcomes are from our illustrative list of objectives for a unit in economics and are numbered accordingly.

Instructional Objective: 2. Understands economic concepts and principles.
Learning Outcome: 2.1 Identifies examples of economic concepts.
1. Which one of the following is an example of commercial credit?
   *A. A manufacturer borrows money to buy raw materials.
   B. A manufacturer borrows money to build a new plant.
   C. A business executive borrows money to build a new house.
   D. A stockbroker borrows money to buy stocks and bonds.

Instructional Objective: 3. Applies economic principles to new situations.
Learning Outcome: 3.2 Predicts the possible outcome of an action involving economic principles.
1. Which one of the following actions of the Federal Reserve Board would most likely contribute to greater inflation?
   *A. Buying government bonds on the open market.
   B. Raising the reserve requirements.
   C. Raising the discount rate.
   D. Lowering the amount of credit granted to member banks.

*Correct answer.

Specifications for Computer Item Banking

Some schools are now preparing pools of objectives and relevant test items for storage in a microcomputer. The items are coded by the specific learning outcome measured, content, grade level, and other relevant characteristics. When such item banks are stored, the computer can be programmed to select items and build a test with known characteristics. The computer will print out these custom-designed tests and also provide scoring, reporting and analyzing functions. The use of microcomputers in the school is relieving teachers of many of the time-consuming functions concerned with classroom testing.

A key feature of computer item banking is that *you get back only what you put in.* If you put in test items that are inappropriate for the objectives being measured or that are technically unsound, the printed test will provide an inadequate measure of the intended learning outcomes. Thus, it is especially important when developing an item bank to use detailed specifications for item writing. Examples of such specifications in several skill areas are presented in Boxes 1, 2, and 3.

---

1. READING

GENERAL INSTRUCTIONAL OBJECTIVE: Comprehends written material.

SPECIFIC LEARNING OUTCOME: Identifies the main thought of a passage.

TYPE OF TEST ITEMS: Multiple-choice (10 items).

READING PASSAGE: One brief paragraph of material that is (1) of interest to children, and (2) at the sixth-grade reading level or lower.

ITEM CHARACTERISTICS: Each test item will contain a stem in the form of a question or incomplete statement, followed by five alternative answers. The *stem* of the item will require the students to identify the main thought in the passage by selecting the word or phrase that best indicates the content of the passage. The *correct response* will be one that contains the central idea of the passage and incorporates the various details included in it. The *incorrect alternatives* (distracters) will contain ideas that are less important than the main thought. They will be made plausible by including content used in the passage and by matching the correct answer in terms of length and grammatical structure. The reading level of the item will be no higher than that of the passage.

Example

(Passage) The koala is a cute, furry animal from Australia. Some of them live in the zoo in San Diego, California. They eat eucalyptus leaves and do not drink water. They are often called "koala bears" but they really aren't bears. They are marsupials, like the kangaroo.

Sample items

This story is mostly about

  A. Australia
  B. bears
*C. koalas
  D. marsupials

---

2. MATH

GENERAL INSTRUCTIONAL OBJECTIVE: Understands our number system.

SPECIFIC LEARNING OUTCOME: Identifies place value.

TYPE OF TEST ITEMS: Multiple-choice (10 items).

ITEM CHARACTERISTICS: Each test item will contain a stem in the form of a question or incomplete statement, followed by four alternative answers. The *stem* of the item will contain a whole number with three to six digits. The student will be asked to identify the value of two of the digits by indicating the degree to which one is a multiple of the other. The *correct response* will indicate an understanding of the place value of both digits. The *incorrect alternatives* (distracters) will consist of common errors in identifying place value.

Sample Item

In the number 9,632, the 9 has a value that is

   A. three times the value of the 3
   B. thirty times the value of the 3
*C. three hundred times the value of the 3
   D. three thousand times the value of the 3

3. WRITING

GENERAL INSTRUCTIONAL OBJECTIVE: Knows fundamentals of written expression.

SPECIFIC LEARNING OUTCOME: Distinguishes between complete and incomplete sentences.

TYPE OF TEST ITEMS: Multiple-choice (10 items).

ITEM CHARACTERISTICS: Each test item will contain one complete sentence and three incomplete sentences. The *stem* of the item will tell the student to choose the complete sentence. The *correct response* will be a complete sentence. The *incorrect alternatives* (distracters) will be sentence fragments.

Sample Item

Choose the *complete* sentence.

   A. The children who went to the zoo.
   B. The monkeys in the zoo swinging.
*C. Going to the zoo was fun.
   D. Whatever you think of the zoo.

Computer item banking is typically a cooperative affair among the teachers in a particular department. The detailed specifications provide greater assurance that a functionally equivalent set of relevant test items will be prepared for each specific learning outcome. The detail is also useful in clarifying the meaning of the test results during test interpretation.

The use of detailed specifications does not mean that the table of specifications, discussed earlier, is to be discarded. It can be used both in planning the overall structure of the item bank and in describing the make-up of the test you want the computer to print for some particular use. In the later case, the table of specifications will help ensure that the printed test provides a balanced measure of the learning outcomes to be evaluated.

In general summary, we can construct an achievement test that provides a relevant and representative measure of our intended learning outcomes by (1) clearly defining our instructional objectives in terms of student performance, (2) preparing an appropriate set of test specifications, and (3) constructing test items that call forth the desired student responses. For more elaborate descriptions of how to construct test items that measure clearly stated learning outcomes see Gronlund (1982, 1985) in the list of references in Appendix C.

Chapter 8

Using Instructional Objectives in Evaluating Performance Skills and Affective Outcomes

There are some learning outcomes in the psychomotor and affective areas that can be measured with the traditional paper-and-pencil test (e.g., knowing the proper procedure, understanding the principles involved). However, for those outcomes that are concerned with actual performance tasks or an individual's typical behavior, we frequently must resort to some type of observational procedure. In evaluating certain performance skills (e.g., making a speech, manipulating laboratory equipment), we need to observe the ongoing performance to judge its effectiveness. In other cases, it is possible to judge performance skill by evaluating the product resulting from the performance (e.g., a theme, painting, wood product). In evaluating student's ability to get along with others or attitudes toward laboratory work, we need to observe them in a variety of situations in which they are likely to reveal their normal behavior. Thus, observational data play an important role in evaluating performance skills and in evaluating those affective outcomes that are reflected in students' typical behavior.

As with testing procedures, the instructional objectives provide the guidelines for preparing appropriate evaluation techniques. Let's take a look at some examples of how evaluation instruments are related to the objectives to be evaluated.

Procedure Evaluation

Observation of procedures is usually guided by a rating scale or check-list. Such instruments provide two important functions. (1) they focus attention on the specific performance to be observed, and (2) they provide a convenient method for recording the judgments of the observer. To be most useful, the instruments should be constructed in accordance with the specific learning outcomes to be evaluated. In fact, if the learning outcomes are clearly specified, the preparation of observational instruments is relatively simple.

Let's assume that the following objectives and set of specific learning outcomes have been specified for a science course.

1. Uses laboratory equipment properly.
   1.1 Selects equipment that is appropriate for a given experiment.
   1.2 Assembles equipment correctly for the experiment.
   1.3 Manipulates equipment as needed during the experiment.
   1.4 Measures accurately with proper measuring device.
   1.5 Follows safety rules in conducting experiment.
   1.6 Uses materials without wasting any.
   1.7 Completes experiment on time.
   1.8 Cleans equipment and returns to proper place.

Each of these specific learning outcomes can serve as an item in a rating scale by simply modifying the wording slightly and by adding a place beneath each item to record the ratings, as shown in Figure 1.

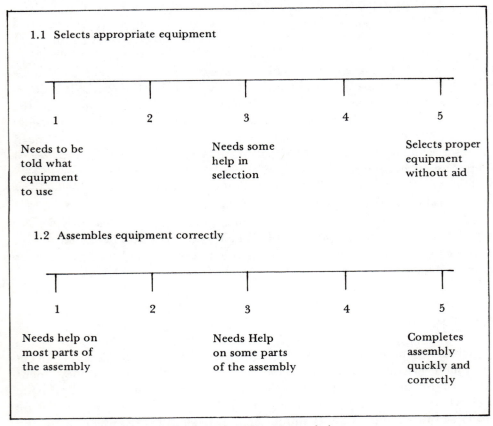

FIGURE 1. Sample rating scale items.

The complete rating scale would, of course, include (1) items covering all specific outcomes to be evaluated, (2) directions for making the ratings, and (3) possibly a place for comments beneath each rating scale item. All we are doing here is illustrating how easy it is to construct a rating scale when the intended outcomes have been clearly specified. The specific learning outcomes indicate the performance to be observed and, thus, become the items in the rating instrument. The graphic scale beneath each item simply provides a place to record the ratings. Using both numbers and descriptive statements to define the points on the scale makes the rating task easier and aids in the interpretation of results.

If a procedure consists of a series of sequential steps and we simply need to judge whether each step has been properly performed, a checklist may be the appropriate evaluation device. For it, we need a description of each specific step and a place to mark whether the performance was satisfactory or not. An illustrative checklist, for evaluating the proper application of varnish, is shown in Figure 2. Note that the task has been broken down into a series of observable elements and that these have been placed in the approximate order in which they are to be performed. The observer then simply checks whether each completed step was satisfactory or unsatisfactory. This "present–absent" type of judgment does not, of course, provide for degrees of proficiency in performing the task. It simply indicates whether an acceptable level of performance has been achieved. To describe levels of proficiency beyond the acceptable minimum we would need to use a more detailed rating system, such as the 5-point scale illustrated earlier.

Product Evaluation

As with procedure evaluation, the evaluation of a product is typically guided by a rating scale or checklist that has been prepared in accordance with the intended outcomes of the performance to be evaluated. Let's assume that an English teacher has specified the following list of outcomes for the writing of a composition.

> 1. Writes effective compositions.
>   1.1 Expresses ideas clearly.
>   1.2 Uses ideas that are logical.
>   1.3 Relates ideas to the main thesis.
>   1.4 Develops the thesis in an organized manner.
>   1.5 Writes well-structured, relevant paragraphs.
>   1.6 Uses parts of speech correctly.
>   1.7 Uses words effectively to convey meaning.
>   1.8 Makes few, or no, spelling errors.
>   1.9 Makes only minor punctuation errors, if any.

The specific learning outcomes listed here define what is meant by an effective composition. Thus, each intended outcome could serve as an item in a checklist, or a rating scale, and the resulting instrument used to evaluate students' compositions.

In some cases, it may be desirable to develop a very detailed list of desired product characteristics, so that the instrument can also be used by students as a guide in preparing the product. The checklist for evaluating a list of instructional objectives, presented in Appendix A, illustrates an instrument that is detailed enough to provide both a guide for the preparation of objectives and a tool for evaluating the final list.

In evaluating some performance skills, both procedure and product may be important. For example, in repairing a malfunctioning automobile engine, we would want the individual to follow a systematic procedure in locating and repairing the malfunction (rather than use trial and error) in addition to producing a smooth-running engine. Similarly, in such areas as typing, cooking, painting, and woodworking, we might want to evaluate both procedure and product. Where this is the case, we, of course, must list the observable elements for both procedure and product and include both in our evaluation

---

DIRECTIONS: On the space in front of each item, place a plus (+) sign if performance was satisfactory, place a minus (−) sign if it was unsatisfactory.

_____ 1. Sands and prepares surface properly.

_____ 2. Wipes dust from surface with appropriate cloth.

_____ 3. Selects appropriate brush.

_____ 4. Selects varnish and checks varnish flow.

_____ 5. Pours needed amount of varnish into clean container.

_____ 6. Puts brush properly into varnish (1/3 of bristle length).

_____ 7. Wipes excess varnish from brush on inside edge of container.

_____ 8. Applies varnish to surface with smooth strokes.

_____ 9. Works from center of surface toward the edges.

_____ 10. Brushes with the grain of the wood.

_____ 11. Uses light strokes to smooth the varnish.

_____ 12. Checks surface for completeness.

_____ 13. Cleans brush with appropriate cleaner.

_____ 14. Does *not* pour excess varnish back into can.

_____ 15. Cleans work area.

FIGURE 2. Checklist for evaluating the proper application of varnish.

instrument. The approach is still the same, however. The specific learning outcomes specify what is to be observed, and the rating scale or checklist merely provides a convenient method of recording our judgments.

Evaluating Affective Outcomes

The same types of obervational instruments used in evaluating performance skills (i.e., rating scales and checklists) can also be used in evaluating outcomes in the affective area. The examples in Figure 3 illustrate how rating scale items might be derived directly from specific learning outcomes in several different affective areas. As with performance evaluation, the key element in preparing the observational instruments is a clearly stated set of intended outcomes.

In addition to observational procedures, affective outcomes are also frequently evaluated with self-report measures. If you want to determine students' attitudes toward school, work, or some particular activity, for example, a self-report device would be useful. Although some information concerning attitude can be gleaned from observation, a self-report inventory provides information that cannot be obtained in any other way. How students feel is a basic element in evaluating attitudes, interests, values, and other types of affective outcomes. The problem is how to get an honest report of those feelings. Obviously, if students fear that their responses will influence their grades, they are likely to distort the results. One solution is to have the students respond anonymously and use only group results to evaluate affective outcomes. Another solution is to reassure students that their responses will not be used against them in any way. Although providing anonymity may be the desired choice for most outcomes, there are times when an individual's responses must be identified in order to provide needed guidance.

The most widely used self-report device by teachers is probably the attitude scale. There are various methods for preparing attitudes scales, but one of the simplest is the Likert method. This involves just two basic steps. (1) Select clearly favorable and clearly unfavorable attitude statements. (2) Provide for responses on the following five-point scale: strongly agree (SA), agree (A), undecided (U), disagree (D), and strongly disagree (SD). An illustrative Likert-type scale for attitude toward a science course is shown in Figure 4.

In scoring favorable statements, like the first item in Figure 4, the five alternatives are given values of 5, 4, 3, 2, 1, going from SA to SD. In scoring unfavorable statements, like the second item in Figure 4, these values are *reversed*. Thus, they are given values of 1, 2, 3, 4, 5, going from SA to SD. An individual's score on this type of scale is the sum of the scores on all items, with a higher score indicating a more favorable attitude.

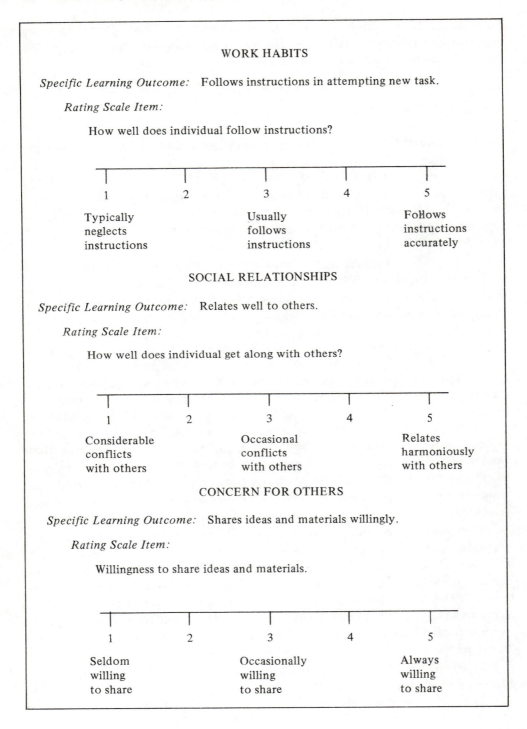

FIGURE 3. Sampling rating scale items for evaluating specific outcomes
in various affective areas.

Directions: Indicate how much you agree or disagree with each statement by circling the appropriate letter(s).

		SA — Strongly Agree
		A — Agree
	KEY	U — Undecided
		D — Disagree
		SD — Strongly Disagree

SA	A	U	D	SD	1. Science classes are interesting.
SA	A	U	D	SD	2. Science laboratory is dull and boring.
SA	A	U	D	SD	3. It is fun working on science problems.
SA	A	U	D	SD	4. Class activities are good.
SA	A	U	D	SD	5. Reading the textbook is a waste of time.
SA	A	U	D	SD	6. The laboratory experiments are interesting.
SA	A	U	D	SD	7. Most class activities are monotonous.
SA	A	U	D	SD	8. I enjoy reading the textbook.
SA	A	U	D	SD	9. The problems we are studying are unimportant.
SA	A	U	D	SD	10. I am *not* very enthusiastic about science.

FIGURE 4. Illustrative Likert-type attitude scale for measuring attitude toward a science course. (Reprinted from N. E. Gronlund, *Measurement and Evaluation in Teaching*, 5th ed., New York, Macmillan, 1985. Used by permission.)

As with other evaluation techniques, the self-report inventory should be prepared in harmony with the outcomes to be evaluated. For example, describing in specific terms what is meant by a "favorable attitude toward science" provides the basis for selecting statements that are clearly favorable and clearly unfavorable. It is then simply a matter of adding the five-point scale to each item and including directions that tell the students how to respond.

In general summary, both performance skills and effective outcomes can be evaluated by using various measurement procedures. We have confined our discussion to brief descriptions of some of the more commonly used observational and self-report techniques to illustrate the important role that clearly specified objectives play in the preparation of such instruments. For more comprehensive descriptions of how to prepare rating scales, checklists, self-report inventories, and other nontest evaluation techniques, consult a standard measurement textbook.

Chapter 9

Using Instructional Objectives in Marking and Reporting

When instructional objectives are stated as learning outcomes, they also provide an excellent basis for marking and reporting. There are several advantages in building the marking and reporting system around a clearly defined list of instructional objectives. (1) The types of performance that students are expected to demonstrate at the end of the instruction are clarified for both students and parents. This provides a guide for the student's own learning activities and increases the likelihood that teachers and parents will not work at cross purposes. (2) This system provides for a diagnostic analysis of the student's strengths and weaknesses. Rather than indicate that a student's achievement is low in particular subject, you can indicate the degree of progress being made toward each of the learning outcomes. (3) Greater continuity is achieved in the instructional program. When teaching, and reporting are all based on the same set of clearly defined objectives, the various aspects of the program are more likely to support and reinforce one another. The test scores and other evaluation results, for example, provide direct evidence for judging and reporting student progress because the evaluation techniques and the report form are both concerned with the same learning outcomes. By the same token the report form provides feedback concerning the teaching and testing. Lack of student progress toward certain learning outcomes, for instance, might suggest the need for instructional changes, improved evaluation techniques, or possibly some modification in the objectives themselves.

Examples of Report Forms Based on Objectives

One of the most highly developed reporting systems, and one that plays an integral role in the instructional program, is that used in the Winnetka

Public Schools. In grades one through eight, there are four Goal Record Cards for each grade level. Each goal card lists the objectives to be achieved by the students in that particular content area. The four areas of study are elementary mathematics, language arts, science, and social studies. A sample Goal Record Card for grade one is shown in Figure 1.

The Winnetka Goal Record Cards serve as basic tools in a program of individualized instruction. Starting in the first grade, each child proceeds through the goals listed on the goal cards of each content area, but not necessarily in the sequence in which they are listed. In grades one and two, progress is checked once or twice a year and check marks are placed after those objectives that have been mastered. From grade three on, a date is entered beside each objective at the time it is achieved. Additional notations are also made when individual work beyond the objectives is completed. Therefore, the goal card provides the student, teacher, and parent with a detailed and continuous picture of the student's learning progress.

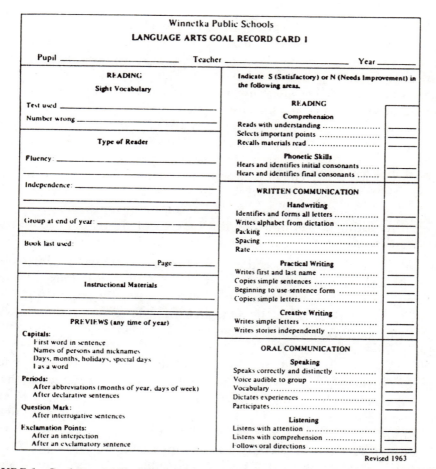

FIGURE 1. Goal Record Card illustrating use of objectives in individualized instruction. (Reproduced by permission of Winnetka Public Schools.)

Many elementary schools use report cards that report learning progress periodically in terms of objectives stated as intended learning outcomes. The following statements illustrate the types of objectives that are commonly listed for grades four to six.

Reading

1. Knows vocabulary.
2. Understands what he or she reads.
3. Locates and uses information effectively.
4. Appreciates good literature.

Mathematics

1. Knows arithmetic facts.
2. Understands basic concepts.
3. Uses fundamental processes.
4. Solves problems involving reasoning.

Sciences

1. Knows specific facts.
2. Understands scientific principles.
3. Applies principles to new situations.

Social Studies

1. Understands basic concepts.
2. Interprets charts, graphs, and maps.
3. Participates effectively in group work.
4. Demonstrates awareness of social problems.

In addition to these areas, the typical report form also includes objectives for listening, speaking, writing, spelling, health, art, music, physical education, and personal and social character traits. Progress in achieving each of the objectives is usually indicated by a letter or a number, which denotes that performance is outstanding (0 or 1), satisfactory (S or 2), or needs improvement (N or 3).

Checklists of objectives are less widely used at the high school level. Their use at the high school level has probably been restricted by the demands of college admissions officers for a single letter grade (A, B, C, D, E) and by the use of these grades for other administrative purposes (awards, scholarships, etc.). There is no reason, of course, why the traditional letter grade cannot be supplemented by a list of instructional objectives. All that is needed is a separate report form for each subject. An example of such a form is shown in Figure 2.

PROGRESS REPORT   **MATHEMATICS**
University of Illinois High School
Urbana, Illinois

―――1st quarter - November ―――― Semester - February ――― 3rd quarter - April ――― Final Report - June

RATING SCALE: *+-Outstanding, S-Satisfactory, U-Unsatisfactory, O-Inadequate basis for judgment*

S U O Respects rights, opinions and abilities of others	+ S U O Evidences independent thought and originality
S U O Accepts responsibility for group's progress	+ S U O Seeks more than superficial knowledge
S U O Is careful with property	+ S U O Understands and applies mathematical principles in problems like those previously studied
S U O Uses time to advantage	
S U O Is attentive	+ S U O Selects and applies principles to new situations
S U O Follows directions	
S U O Makes regular preparations as required	+ S U O Performs arithmetic operations
	+ S U O Performs algebraic operations
	+ S U O Does written work carefully

ACHIEVEMENT	EFFORT
The grade below is a measure of achievement with respect to what is expected of a pupil of this class in this school, and in relation to what is expected in the next higher course in this subject.	The grade below is an estimate, based on evidence available to the teacher, of the individual student's effort.
―――*5 excellent* ―――*2 passing, but weak*	―――*5 excellent* ―――*2 weak*
―――*4 very good* ―――*1 failing*	―――*4 very good* ―――*1 very weak*
―――*3 creditable* ―――*0 inadequate basis for judgment*	―――*3 creditable* ―――*0 inadequate basis for judgment*

COMMENTS:

Teacher:_____

FIGURE 2. Report form illustrating use of checklists of objectives at high school level. (Reproduced by permission of University High School, Urbana, Ill.)

Note on this form that there are two sets of objectives. At the upper left are the common objectives that appear on all report forms. At the upper right are the objectives that are unique to the particular content area, in this case, mathematics. Note also that provisions are made for giving a separate grade in achievement and effort (which prevents contamination of the achievement grade). A report form such as this makes it possible to assign a single achievement grade that is useful for administrative purposes and at the same time to provide students and parents with a detailed report of student progress toward the general goals of the school and the specific objectives of the course.

Steps in Preparing Report Forms Based on Objectives

A report form based on a checklist of objectives is most likely to serve its intended function when it is developed cooperatively. The teachers who are intimately acquainted with the instructional program are probably in the best position to identify and to state the original list of objectives. However, students and parents should also participate in the preparation of the form because they must be able to comprehend it.

The following steps outline the general procedure for developing a report form based on a checklist of objectives (Gronlund, 1974).

1. Identify and State a Tentative List of Instructional Objectives to Be Included in the Report Form. This can be done by committees of teachers organized by content area. Teachers at each of the grade levels covered by the report form should be included on the committees. Students and parents might also be included on these committees, if possible. The tentative list of objectives developed by these committees should, of course, be those that most adequately reflect the general goals of the school and the specific goals of each instructional area.

2. Narrow Down the Tentative List to the Several Most Appropriate Objectives in Each Instructional Area. Including all instructional objectives in each area is, of course, impossible because it would result in a long, unmanageable list that would only tend to confuse the users of the report. There are several bases for selecting the objectives to be included. First, there is the importance of the objective. It should be considered a basic learning outcome in the area (e.g., reasoning ability in mathematics). Second, it should be an outcome that occurs at all of the grade levels covered by the report. Since each report form typically covers several grade levels, only those objectives that are common to all levels should be included. Some report forms leave a few blank spaces for each content area, so that additional objectives can be added by any teacher using the report. Third, the outcome should be one for which it is possible to obtain sound evaluation data. Checklists of objectives are sometimes criticized because they are so difficult to mark. The assumption, of course, is that our tests and other evaluation instruments are designed to provide evidence of student progress toward these particular objectives. The report form merely provides a convenient place to record the judgments that are derived from the evaluation data. If there is no evaluation data on which to base the judgments, the checklists are indeed difficult to mark. Fourth, outcome should be clear to students, parents, and other users of the reports. Lack of clarity would not necessarily result in the elimination of an objective, but it might call for considerable modification in the wording.

3. Present a Tentative Copy of the Report Form to School Personnel, Students, and Parents for Revision and Adoption. Those who have not participated up to this point in the preparation of the report form should be offered an opportunity to review the form and to suggest improvements. A review by persons who have not seen the report during its development is especially good for detecting ambiguity and any unnecessary complexity in the statements of the objectives. It also provides an excellent opportunity to acquaint school personnel, students, and parents with the function of the report from and its role in the instructional program.

4. Try Out the Tentative Report Form and Revise as Needed. During the trial period, collect suggestions from teachers for simplifying the procedures and mechanics for filling out the forms. Similarly, collect suggestions and criticisms from students and parents concerning the clarity and usefulness of the reports. At the end of the trial period, revise the report form as needed.

During the development of the report form and throughout its various revisions, keep in mind that the final checklist of objectives must be in harmony with those of the instructional program. This does not mean, however, that radical changes in the original list of objectives cannot be made. Discussions of the objectives in the tentative report form frequently suggest needed revisions in the instructional objectives of the school and consequently in the instructional program itself.

To summarize, the same objectives that direct the teaching and testing activities in the instructional program should provide the basis for reporting student progress. Including checklists of instructional objectives on the report form communicates to both students and parents the nature of the expected learning outcomes, provides a diagnostic picture of learning progress, and provides for greater continuity in the instructional program. To be most effective, such report forms should be developed cooperatively by teachers, other school personnel, students, and parents.

A Final Note

Throughout this book we have emphasized the importance of stating instructional objectives as learning outcomes and of defining each objective in terms of observable student performance. The procedures for preparing, selecting, and using clearly defined objectives have been described and illustrated. Ideally, this approach would permeate the entire school system, with committees of teachers identifying the common instructional objectives for each content area and the unique objectives for each particular course or instructional unit. This ideal is seldom approached, however. Therefore, the chances are good that you will find yourself teaching in a school that does not have this broad emphasis on well-defined objectives. What should you do in this situation? Well, for one thing, you can identify and define instructional objectives for each of the courses or instructional units that you are teaching. This will guide you in selecting instructional materials and methods, in preparing tests and other evaluating instruments, and in reporting student progress toward the desired learning outcomes. Even if the school uses a traditional marking system (e.g., A, B, C, D, E), your checklist of objectives for each course can be used as a reporting guide during student-teacher and parent-teacher conferences, and as a basis for determining the students' letter grades or other marks.

The goal card that was illustrated earlier in this chapter provides a convenient means of recording the final list of objectives and a useful instructional device. It can be used both for directing the learning activities of students and for making informal reports of their learning progress. If placed in the hands of students, the goal card can also serve as a learning guide. It will clarify for students the desired learning outcomes, help them identify their own strengths and weaknesses in learning, and enhance the development of their self-evaluation skills.

Appendix A

Checklist for Evaluating
the Final List of Objectives

In the first four chapters, we told how to identify and define instructional objectives in terms of student performance. Our focus was on the *stating* of the objectives and the specific learning outcomes. Questions such as "Which objectives are most desirable for a particular instructional unit?" we leave to the curriculum specialist and subject expert. In evaluating your final list of objectives, however, you might want to appraise the adequacy of the list, as well as how clearly the statements indicate your instructional intent. Therefore, general criteria for evaluating the final list of objectives and specific learning outcomes have been incorporated into this checklist.

This checklist is intended as a diagnostic tool for detecting and correcting errors in the final list of objectives. Any negative answer indicates an area where improvement is needed. The checklist is also useful, of course, as a guide for developing the original list of instructional objectives.

CHECKLIST

	Yes	No

Adequacy of the List of General Instructional Objectives

1. Does each general instructional objective indicate an appropriate outcome for the instructional unit? (See recommendations of curriculum and subject experts.) _____ _____
2. Does the list of general instructional objectives include all logical outcomes of the unit (knowledge, understanding, skills, attitudes, etc.)? _____ _____
3. Are the general instructional objectives attainable (do they take into account the ability of the students, facilities, time available, etc.)? _____ _____

	Yes	No

4. Are the general instructional objectives in harmony with the philosophy of the school? _____ _____

5. Are the general instructional objectives in harmony with sound principles of learning (e.g., are the outcomes those that are most permanent and transferrable)? _____ _____

Statements of General Instructional Objectives

6. Does each general instructional objective begin with a *verb* (e.g., knows, understands, appreciates, etc.)? _____ _____

7. Is each general instructional objective stated in terms of *student performance* (rather than teacher performance)? _____ _____

8. Is each general instructional objective stated as a learning product (rather than in terms of the learning process)? _____ _____

9. Is each general instructional objective stated in terms of the students' *terminal performance* (rather than the subject matter to be covered)? _____ _____

10. Does each general instructional objective include only one general learning outcome? _____ _____

11. Is each general instructional objective stated at the proper level of generality (i.e., is it clear, concise, and readily definable)? _____ _____

12. Is each general instructional objective stated so that it is relatively independent (i.e., free from overlap with other objectives)? _____ _____

Statements of Specific Learning Outcomes

13. Is each general instructional objective defined by a list of specific learning outcomes that describes the types of performance students are expected to demonstrate? _____ _____

14. Does each specific learning outcome begin with a *verb* that specifies definite, *observable performance* (e.g., identifies, describes, lists, etc.)? _____ _____

15. Is the performance described in each specific learning outcome relevant to the general instructional objective? _____ _____

16. Is there a sufficient number of specific learning outcomes to describe adequately the performance of students who have achieved each of the general instructional objectives? _____ _____

17. Is each specific learning outcome sufficiently free of course content so that it can be used with various units of study? _____ _____

Appendix B

Illustrative Verbs

Illustrative Verbs for Stating General Instructional Objectives

Analyze	Compute	Interpret	Perform	Translate
Apply	Create	Know	Recognize	Understand
Appreciate	Demonstrate	Listen	Speak	Use
Comprehend	Evaluate	Locate	Think	Write

Illustrative Verbs for Stating Specific Learning Outcomes[2]

"Creative" Behaviors

Alter	Paraphrase	Reconstruct	Rephrase	Rewrite
Ask	Predict	Regroup	Restate	Simplify
Change	Question	Rename	Restructure	Synthesize
Design	Rearrange	Reorganize	Retell	Systematize
Generalize	Recombine	Reorder	Revise	Vary
Modify				

Complex, Logical, Judgmental Behaviors

Analyze	Conclude	Deduce	Formulate	Plan
Appraise	Contrast	Defend	Generate	Structure
Combine	Criticize	Evaluate	Induce	Substitute
Compare	Decide	Explain	Infer	

---

[1]This list was developed by Calvin K. Claus, Psychology Department, National College of Education, Evanston, Ill. Printed by permission from a paper presented at the annual meeting of the National Council on Measurement in Education (Chicago: February, 1968).

General Discriminative Behaviors

Choose	Detect	Identify	Match	Place
Collect	Differentiate	Indicate	Omit	Point
Define	Discriminate	Isolate	Order	Select
Describe	Distinguish	List	Pick	Separate

Social Behaviors

Accept	Communicate	Discuss	Invite	Praise
Agree	Compliment	Excuse	Join	React
Aid	Contribute	Forgive	Laugh	Smile
Allow	Cooperate	Greet	Meet	Talk
Answer	Dance	Help	Participate	Thank
Argue	Disagree	Interact	Permit	Volunteer

Language Behaviors

Abbreviate	Edit	Punctuate	Speak	Tell
Accent	Hyphenate	Read	Spell	Translate
Alphabetize	Indent	Recite	State	Verbalize
Articulate	Outline	Say	Summarize	Whisper
Call	Print	Sign	Syllabify	Write
Capitalize	Pronounce			

"Study" Behaviors

Arrange	Compile	Itemize	Mark	Record
Categorize	Copy	Label	Name	Reproduce
Chart	Diagram	Locate	Note	Search
Cite	Find	Look	Organize	Sort
Circle	Follow	Map	Quote	Underline

Music Behaviors

Blow	Compose	Hum	Pluck	Strum
Bow	Finger	Mute	Practice	Tap
Clap	Harmonize	Play	Sing	Whistle

Physical Behaviors

Arch	Bend	Catch	Climb	Float
Bat	Carry	Chase	Face	Grab
Grasp	Kick	Pull	Skip	Swim
Grip	Knock	Push	Somersault	Swing
Hit	Lift	Run	Stand	Throw
Hop	March	Skate	Step	Toss
Jump	Pitch	Ski	Stretch	Walk

Arts Behaviors

Assemble	Dot	Illustrate	Press	Stamp
Blend	Draw	Melt	Roll	Stick
Brush	Drill	Mix	Rub	Stir
Build	Fold	Mold	Sand	Trace
Carve	Form	Nail	Saw	Trim
Color	Frame	Paint	Sculpt	Varnish
Construct	Hammer	Paste	Shake	Wipe
Cut	Handle	Pat	Sketch	Wrap
Dab	Heat	Pour	Smooth	

Drama Behaviors

Act	Display	Express	Pass	Show
Clasp	Emit	Leave	Perform	Sit
Cross	Enter	Move	Proceed	Start
Direct	Exit	Pantomime	Respond	Turn

Mathematical Behaviors

Add	Derive	Group	Number	Square
Bisect	Divide	Integrate	Plot	Subtract
Calculate	Estimate	Interpolate	Prove	Tabulate
Check	Extrapolate	Measure	Reduce	Tally
Compute	Extract	Multiply	Solve	Verify
Count	Graph			

Laboratory Science Behaviors

Apply	Demonstrate	Keep	Prepare	Specify
Calibrate	Dissect	Lengthen	Remove	Straighten
Conduct	Feed	Limit	Replace	Time
Connect	Grow	Manipulate	Report	Transfer
Convert	Increase	Operate	Reset	Weigh
Decrease	Insert	Plant	Set	

General Appearance, Health, and Safety Behaviors

Button	Dress	Fasten	Taste	Unzip
Clean	Drink	Fill	Tie	Wait
Clear	Eat	Go	Unbutton	Wash
Close	Eliminate	Lace	Uncover	Wear
Comb	Empty	Stop	Untie	Zip
Cover				

Miscellaneous

Aim	Erase	Lead	Relate	Stake
Attempt	Expand	Lend	Repeat	Start
Attend	Extend	Let	Return	Stock
Begin	Feel	Light	Ride	Store
Bring	Finish	Make	Rip	Strike
Buy	Fit	Mend	Save	Suggest
Come	Fix	Miss	Scratch	Supply
Complete	Flip	Offer	Send	Support
Consider	Get	Open	Serve	Switch
Correct	Give	Pack	Sew	Take
Crease	Grind	Pay	Share	Tear
Crush	Guide	Peel	Sharpen	Touch
Designate	Hand	Pin	Shoot	Try
Determine	Hang	Position	Shorten	Twist
Develop	Hold	Present	Shovel	Type
Discover	Hook	Produce	Shut	Use
Distribute	Hunt	Propose	Signify	Vote
Do	Include	Provide	Slip	Watch
Drop	Inform	Put	Slide	Weave
End	Lay	Raise	Spread	Work

Appendix C

References

Bloom, B. S., ed., et al. *Taxonomy of Educational Objectives: Handbook I, Cognitive Domain.* New York: David Mckay Co., Inc., 1956. Describes the cognitive categories in detail and presents illustrative objectives and test items for each.

Gronlund, N. E. *Constructing Achievement Tests,* 3rd ed. Englewood Cliffs, N.J.: Prentice-Hall, Inc., 1982. Describes and illustrates how to construct test items that measure learning outcomes at the various levels of the cognitive domain of the *Taxonomy of Educational Objectives.*

Gronlund, N. E. *Improving Marking and Reporting in Classroom Instruction.* New York: Macmillan Publishing Co., Inc., 1974. A brief practical guide (58 pages) describing and illustrating both criterion-referenced and norm-referenced marking practices.

Gronlund, N. E. *Measurement and Evaluation in Teaching,* 5th ed. New York: Macmillan Publishing Co., Inc., 1985. A textbook that describes in more comprehensive form the process of preparing instructional objectives and using them in testing and evaluating student learning.

Harrow, A. J. *A Taxonomy of the Psychomotor Domain.* New York: David McKay Co., Inc., 1972. Provides a model for classifying learning outcomes in the psychomotor domain and presents illustrative objectives.

Krathwohl, D. R., ed., et al. *Taxonomy of Educational Objectives: Handbook II, Affective Domain.* New York: David McKay Co., Inc., 1964. Describes the affective categories in detail and presents illustrative objectives and test items for each.

Simpson, E. J. "The Classification of Educational Objectives in the Psychomotor Domain." *The Psychomotor Domain.* Vol. 3. Washington: Gryphon House, 1972. Describes the psychomotor domain in detail and presents illustrative objectives.

Index

ISBN 0-02-348000-9